photography by Martin Brigdale

QUADRILLE

michel roux

pastry

SAVOURY & SWEET

notes
All spoon measures are level unless otherwise
stated: 1tsp = 5ml spoon; 1tbsp = 15ml spoon.

Use fresh herbs, sea salt and freshly ground
black pepper unless otherwise suggested.

Egg sizes are given where they are critical,
otherwise use medium eggs, preferably organic
or free-range. Anyone who is pregnant or in a
vulnerable health group should avoid recipes that
use raw egg whites or lightly cooked eggs.

Timings are for fan-assisted ovens. If using a
conventional oven, increase the temperature by
15°C (1 Gas mark). Use an oven thermometer
to check the temperature.

Editorial director **Anne Furniss**
Creative director **Mary Evans**
Project editor **Janet Illsley**
Translator and editor **Kate Whiteman**
Photographer **Martin Brigdale**
Props stylist **Helen Trent**
Production director **Vincent Smith**
Senior Production controller **Ruth Deary**

First published in 2008 by
Quadrille Publishing Limited
Alhambra House
27-31 Charing Cross Road
London WC2H 0LS
www.quadrille.co.uk

Text © 2008 Michel Roux
Photography © 2008 Martin Brigdale
Design and layout © 2008 Quadrille Publishing Limited

ISBN 978 184400 620 5

Printed in Singapore

To all young cooks to encourage them in the art of pastry-making

At the age of fourteen, under the tutelage of my apprentice master in Paris, Monsieur Loyal, I was introduced to the all-important craft of the *tourier* who is responsible for preparing, rolling and shaping the dough – the foundation stone of all pastry-making. Starting each morning at 4am, 6 days a week, I gradually discovered this extraordinary world and the fascination has stayed with me ever since.

At that early hour, the silence was almost oppressive, only broken by the monotonous, timid ticking of the clock on the bakery wall, and the occasional clunk of our rolling pins as we laid them down between rolling out different pastries. Our constant companions, always within reach, were brushes for dusting off excess flour from the work surface, and pastry cutters of every description.

Working on the *tour* – the chilled slab from which the *tourier* takes his name – we would turn out one kind of pastry after another, always in the same order: croissants, brioches, puff pastry, flan pastry, *pâte brisée*, *pâte sucrée* and so on … a veritable festival of pastry! The smell of those pastries made me so hungry that I couldn't resist nibbling a piece of raw dough – an indefinable, reassuring pleasure.

At the break of dawn, a little light would seep through the verandah that served as our roof. This signalled a certain ritual. Monsieur Loyal would utter his first words of the day, breaking the silence, 'Turn off the light, little one'. I obeyed the order promptly, switching off the fluorescent tubes suspended on chains above our heads, and revealing the veil of flour floating in the atmosphere like morning mist. It was time to finish our work on the *tour*, leaving the pastry we had prepared over the past few hours for others to garnish and bake. I was only a kid but I felt serenely happy, and I grew to love the craft of pastry more each day.

In writing this book, my aim is to pass on the secrets I have learnt about pastry-making from such an early age. Over the years I have honed my skills and discovered so much more to reveal. You might say it is no longer a necessary skill, that you can buy ready-made pastries from the supermarket, but these are nowhere near as good as 'the real thing' and many of them contain lots of additives – just take a look at the packets.

All of the pastries in this book can be made in an electric mixer but as a purist, I prefer the artisan approach, working by hand where appropriate, and I urge you to join me in pastry-making in its purest form.

the main ingredients

In pastry-making, as in all cooking, you will only achieve a result to be proud of if the ingredients you use are of excellent quality. Pastry requires very few ingredients, so it is particularly important to choose them carefully.

Flour The most commonly used plain flour for pastry-making in France is type 45, which is often called pastry flour. Finer and whiter than French type 55, it contains less fibre and is perfect for puff pastry and leavening rich doughs, like brioche. Type 55 flour has a high gluten content, which adds elasticity to the dough, so it is generally used for pizzas, and sometimes also for *pâte sablée* and *pâte sucrée*. In certain cases, it is also used for raised pie pastry and can on occasion be used for tart cases. You can, of course, use standard plain flour, or bread flour rather than type 55, but you can obtain these special flours from specialist suppliers (see page 297).

Humidity is the enemy of flour encouraging mould and bacteria, so always store your flour in a dry place. Once the original packaging is opened, transfer the flour to an airtight storage jar.

Fats I much prefer butter to margarine, which leaves an unpleasant taste on the palate and to my mind is a false economy. 'Dry butter', such as Charentes Lescure, which contains less than 16% and preferably only 10% water is particularly good for puff pastry. Occasionally, for a change, it's nice to use salted butter for *pâte sablée*. Whichever variety you choose, always taste a bit of plain butter before using it – to ensure that it tastes fresh and not remotely rancid.

Eggs Always choose free-range eggs. Avoid battery eggs like the plague – they should be banned, and fortunately will be in Britain by 2012. The shell is a natural barrier against microbes, and I would advise you not to use eggs with cracked or broken shells.

Store eggs pointed end down in the fridge, in the egg compartment or their original box and take them out of the fridge an hour or two before using. In most of Europe, the date of lay will be printed on the box. Never use eggs that are more than 28 days old and always respect the 'use by' date if printed on the egg.

Sugar Caster sugar and to a lesser extent icing sugar are most commonly used in pastry. Sugar hates humidity, which causes it to crystallise or form lumps, so once you have opened the packet transfer it to an airtight jar or plastic container.

Spices All spices – paprika, cayenne, ginger, saffron, cinnamon etc – rapidly lose their savour once the jar is open, so respect the 'use by' date and replenish your stocks regularly.

rolling out pastry
Lightly dust your work surface (ideally marble) and rolling pin with flour. Using light strokes and applying even pressure, roll out the pastry, giving it a quarter turn and flipping it over from time to time. This will prevent it from sticking and helps to keep it aerated. Continue until the pastry is the size and shape required.

lining a flan tin (or ring)

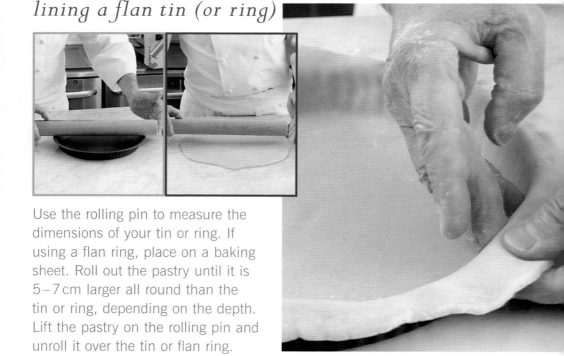

Use the rolling pin to measure the dimensions of your tin or ring. If using a flan ring, place on a baking sheet. Roll out the pastry until it is 5–7 cm larger all round than the tin or ring, depending on the depth. Lift the pastry on the rolling pin and unroll it over the tin or flan ring.

Lightly press the pastry into the edges of the tin and into the flutes (if appropriate).

Each chapter starts with a step-by-step guide to preparing the particular dough. Here I am focusing on general techniques that apply to many of the pastries in the book. A cool kitchen is the key to successful pastry-making.

Trim off excess pastry with a knife, or by rolling the pin over the tin. Press a ball of pastry around the sides to lift the edges slightly. Rest the pastry case in the fridge for 20 minutes or so to avoid shrinkage during baking.

Prick all over the pastry base with a fork, to release trapped air, before baking blind or filling directly, as suggested in the recipe.

baking blind

Line the flan case with baking parchment or greaseproof paper
and fill with a layer of baking beans (either ceramic beans or dried
pulses) to weight the pastry down and prevent it from rising unevenly.
Bake 'blind' in the oven at the temperature given in the recipe (usually
180–190°C) for the specified time, then remove the paper and beans
and return to the oven to dry and colour the base. If the pastry case
won't be returning to the oven to bake the filling, it will need to
be cooked completely.

Using a suitable sized pastry cutter or a plate as a guide, cut out rounds to line your individual flan or tartlet tins. Depending on the depth of the tins, the pastry will need to be 4–7 cm larger in diameter than the tins. Place the pastry discs in the tins and use your thumbs to ease the pastry in, pushing it up gently to create a slightly raised edge.

Individual pastry cases can be lined with paper and beans in the same way (see left), or instead you can place a flan tin of the same size inside the pastry case to bake it blind. Again, you will need to return the pastry cases to the oven for 5–10 minutes after removing the 'lining tin' to colour and dry the bases.

pastry borders

To give a flan (or pie) a neat, decorative border, you can either use a special crimping tool to pinch the raised edge (below right), or crimp the edge by hand.

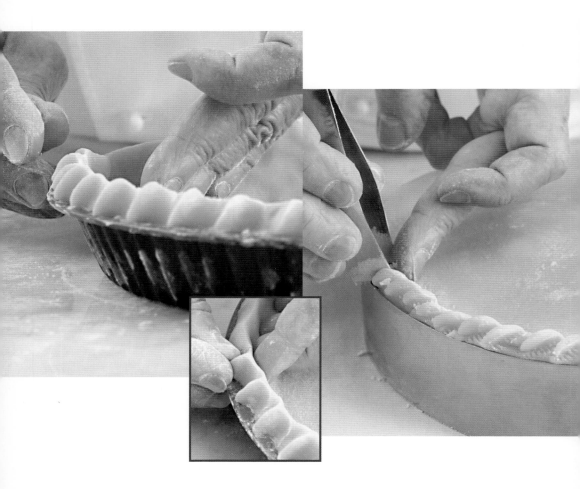

To do this, push the fingers of one hand into the inside rim of the pastry while gently pinching the outer edge of the pastry between the thumb and index finger of your other hand. Repeat evenly all around the edge.

Scoring pastry can give a lovely finish and you can create appropriate patterns – to resemble fish scales, for example, it you are preparing a fish en croûte.

Brush the pastry with egg wash first. Holding the knife at a slight angle, score one-third or halfway into the pastry, never right through. If you cut straight down, the pastry (especially puff) is liable to gape. To form fish scales, use a flicking action. After baking, brush with clarified butter to give a shiny finish.

applied pastry decorations

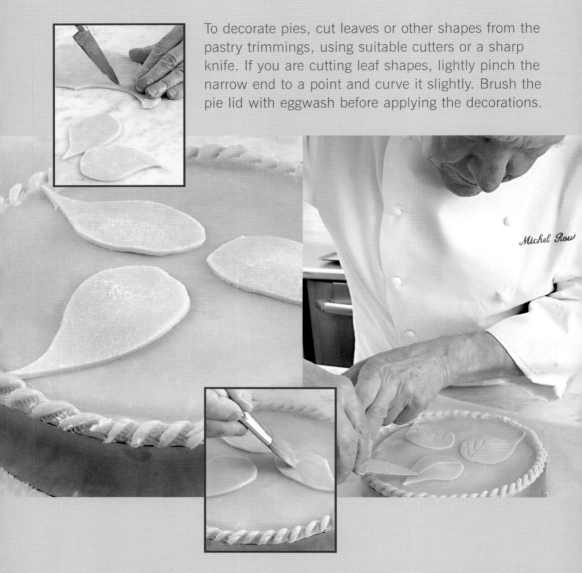

To decorate pies, cut leaves or other shapes from the pastry trimmings, using suitable cutters or a sharp knife. If you are cutting leaf shapes, lightly pinch the narrow end to a point and curve it slightly. Brush the pie lid with eggwash before applying the decorations.

Once you have positioned the decorations on the pie, brush them with eggwash. If using leaves, mark veins with the tip of the knife.

You can create a lattice by criss-crossing pastry strips over a flan or pie, but a lattice roller will give a finer, neater finish. Simply roll out the pastry to a square or rectangle large enough to cover the flan or pie. Now, starting at one side, roll the lattice cutter firmly over the pastry, making sure you cut right through. Repeat to cut the rest of the pastry in the same direction (making sure you are not overlapping the first cuts).

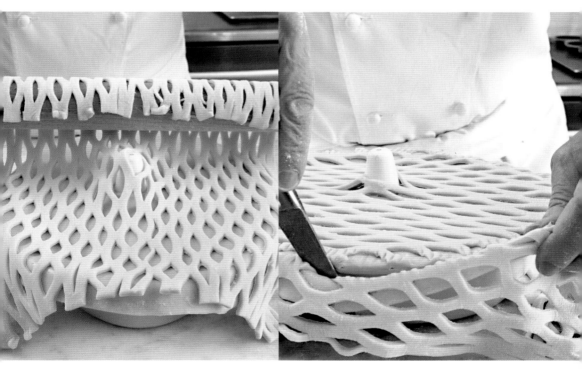

Now lift the pastry, gently teasing it apart to open out the lattice. Wrap around the rolling pin and carefully lift over the flan or glazed pie. Trim off the excess pastry and brush the lattice with eggwash before baking.

Pâte brisée and flan pastry (pâte à foncer) are versatile pastries, used for all kinds of bases. Largely interchangeable in cooking, both can be made successfully in an electric mixer fitted with a dough hook. It certainly makes the job simpler and saves time, but I prefer to make them by hand on a cold work surface. My favourite is the more delicate pâte brisée — with its crumbly crunch it makes the perfect base for a lemon tart. But when tarts and quiches need to be made several hours in advance, I would choose pâte à foncer.

To make a perfect lining for pastry rings and tart tins, both of these pastries must be rolled out as thinly as possible (3–4 mm thickness), to ensure that the pastry base is properly cooked and is light, crisp and digestible. Then the choice of filling is down to you — give your imagination free rein!

shortcrust pastries

pâte brisée

makes about 450g

This pastry is more delicate, crumbly and lighter than flan pastry.

250g plain flour
150g butter, cut into small pieces and
    slightly softened
1 tsp fine salt
pinch of caster sugar
1 egg
1 tbsp cold milk

Heap the flour on a work surface and make a well. Put in the butter, salt, sugar and egg. Using your fingertips, mix and cream these ingredients together.

Little by little, draw in the flour, working the dough delicately until it has a grainy texture.

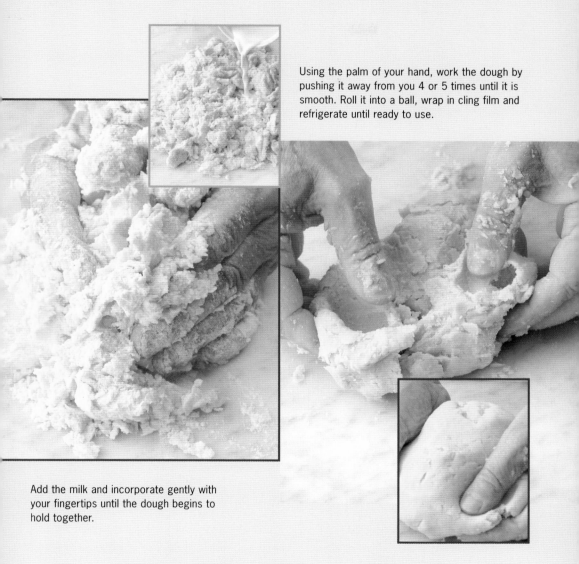

Using the palm of your hand, work the dough by pushing it away from you 4 or 5 times until it is smooth. Roll it into a ball, wrap in cling film and refrigerate until ready to use.

Add the milk and incorporate gently with your fingertips until the dough begins to hold together.

Pâte brisée will keep perfectly in an airtight container in the fridge for a week or up to 3 months in the freezer.

flan pastry

Known as *pâte à foncer* in France,
this pastry is less delicate and fragile than
pâte brisée, but it tastes just as good and has
a crisper texture. It can be kept in the fridge for a
week or in the freezer for up to 3 months.

250g plain flour
125g butter, cut into small pieces and slightly softened
1 egg
1 tsp caster sugar
$1/2$ tsp fine salt
40ml cold water

Heap the flour on the work surface and make a well. Put the butter, egg, sugar and salt in the middle. With your fingertips, mix and cream the ingredients in the well.

Now, little by little, draw the flour into the centre and work the dough with your fingertips to a grainy texture. Add the cold water and mix it in until the dough begins to hold together.

Using the palm of your hand, push the dough away from you 4 or 5 times until it is smooth. Roll the pastry into a ball, wrap in cling film and refrigerate until ready to use.

These basic pastries can be used to create all kinds of savoury and sweet tarts. Simply roll out the pastry to a 3mm thickness and use to line a lightly greased 20–23cm diameter flan ring (see pages 10–11) or 6 individual flan tins, 10–12cm in diameter. Rest in the fridge for 20 minutes. Prick the bases. Bake blind at 190°C/Gas 5 for 20 minutes (allow 10 minutes for individual flans), following the instructions on pages 12–13. Remove the beans and paper (or lining tins), then return the pastry case to the oven for 15 minutes (or 5 minutes for individual flans) until completely cooked. Cool on a wire rack. Either use at once or leave until cold, then wrap in cling film and freeze for up to 2 weeks. Take out of the freezer about 20 minutes before filling. Each of the following will serve 6–10.

Ricotta tart Flavour some sieved ricotta cheese with freshly chopped herbs, diced tomatoes, a little finely chopped onion and a drizzle of olive oil. Season with salt and pepper to taste and use to fill the pastry case. Decorate with chopped herbs or sprigs.

Mascarpone and courgette tart Flavour some mascarpone with a little finely grated fresh ginger and spread it over the base of the pastry case. Arrange lightly grilled courgette rounds on top and sprinkle with a few drops of balsamic vinegar.

Tuna and avocado tart Wash a few handfuls of small spinach leaves, pat dry and spread over the base of the pastry case. Dress avocado slices lightly with lemon juice and arrange over the spinach. Scatter over some flaked tuna (canned in oil). Top with chopped hard-boiled eggs mixed with chopped coriander leaves.

Seasonal fruit tart Choose whichever fruits are ripe and at their seasonal best – pears, apricots, plums, peaches and cherries are particularly good. Poach them in sugar syrup (see page 291) until just tender, then drain and let cool. Spread a layer of crème pâtissière (see page 292) over the tart base and arrange the fruits on top. If you like, boil the sugar syrup to reduce down to a glaze and brush over the fruit.

quiches lorraine

serves 6

375g pâte brisée (see pages 20–1)
140g lightly salted fatty pork belly
1 egg
3 egg yolks
300 ml double cream
pinch of freshly grated nutmeg
salt and freshly ground pepper
140g Gruyère or Comté, freshly grated

Roll out the pastry to a 2 mm thickness. Using a 16 cm cutter or plate as a guide, cut out 6 rounds. Use these to line 6 individual loose-bottomed quiche tins, 10 cm in diameter and 3 cm deep (see page 13). Chill for 20 minutes.

Preheat the oven to 190°C / Gas 5. Prick the pastry case bases. Bake the cases blind, following the instructions on page 13, for 15 minutes. Lower the oven setting to 170°C / Gas 3. Remove the beans and paper (or lining tins) and return the pastry cases to the oven for 5 minutes. Leave in the tins and set aside while you prepare the filling.

Cook the pork belly in boiling water for about 20 minutes, then drain and cut into small lardons and leave to cool.

Put the whole egg and yolks in a bowl, mix in the cream with a whisk and season with the nutmeg and salt and pepper. Divide the lardons and grated cheese between the pastry cases, then fill to the brim with the egg mixture. Bake in the oven for 15 minutes.

Unmould the quiches onto a wire rack, then transfer to individual plates and serve.

A salad of frisée with some garlicky croûtons is the perfect accompaniment to these delicate little quiches. For a vegetarian option, replace the lardons with sautéed, chopped button mushrooms.

This elegant tart tastes as good as it looks. It takes a little while to prepare, but is well worth the effort. Serve it barely warm.

340g pâte brisée (see pages 20–1)
48 medium asparagus spears
salt and freshly ground pepper
5 semi-confit red peppers, about 600g
  in total, (see page 289)

1 egg
2 egg yolks
200ml double cream
pinch of freshly grated nutmeg
8 dill sprigs

Roll out the pastry to a 3mm thickness and use it to line a loose-bottomed oblong tart tin (tranche tin), measuring 35 x 11cm and 2.5cm deep (see pages 10–11). Chill for about 20 minutes.

Preheat the oven to 190°C/Gas 5. Prick the base of the pastry case. Bake the case blind, following the instructions on page 12, for 20 minutes. Lower the oven setting to 170°C/Gas 3. Remove the beans and paper and return the pastry case to the oven for 10 minutes. Leave in the tin and set aside while you prepare the filling.

Cook the asparagus in boiling salted water until just tender. Drain, refresh, then drain thoroughly and pat dry. Trim the asparagus spears to the width of the tin (11cm).

Finely dice the peppers, drain well and pat with kitchen paper to sponge off the oil they absorb during the confit process. Scatter them in an even layer in the pastry case.

Mix the whole egg, yolks and cream together in a bowl using a whisk and season with a little nutmeg, salt and pepper. Pour three-quarters of the mixture over the peppers. Lay the asparagus spears over the peppers, tip to tail in pairs along the length of the tin.

Carefully spoon the remaining egg mixture over the asparagus. Immediately bake the tart for 30 minutes. Slide onto a wire rack and leave for 20 minutes before unmoulding.

Use a palette knife to lift the flan onto a serving platter. Garnish with the dill and serve warm. Use a knife with a long, very sharp blade to slice the flan.

potato pie

serves 8

Serve with a salad of watercress and treviso or radicchio.
Any leftover pie will be delicious eaten cold.

400g pâte brisée (see pages 20–1)
100g butter
1.5kg potatoes (preferably King Edward),
   peeled and cut into 3mm thick slices
225g onions, thinly sliced
salt and freshly ground pepper

4 tbsp mixed chopped flat leaf parsley
  and tarragon
pinch of freshly grated nutmeg
eggwash (1 egg yolk mixed with 1 tbsp milk)
200ml double cream

Heat the butter in a large frying pan and cook the potatoes and onions, stirring often, over a medium heat for 5–6 minutes until the potatoes are pliable and one-third cooked. Season and mix in the herbs and nutmeg. Tip into a colander to drain; leave until cold.

Roll out two-thirds of the pastry to a round, 3mm thick. Use to line a lightly greased 22cm diameter (4cm deep) flan ring (see pages 10–11). Chill for 20 minutes.

Preheat the oven to 180°C/Gas 4. Lightly prick the pastry base, then spread the potatoes evenly in the pastry case.

Roll out the rest of the pastry to a 23–24cm disc. Brush the edge of the pastry case with eggwash. Roll the pastry disc loosely around the rolling pin and unroll it over the potatoes. Trim off excess pastry and crimp the edges at 2–3mm intervals to seal and make a border. Roll out the trimmings and cut out leaves (see page 16). Brush the top of the pie with eggwash and arrange the leaves on top. Brush them with eggwash and draw 'veins' with a knife tip. Use the knife tip to cut out a small 'chimney' in the centre of the lid, then insert a small funnel of rolled-up foil to let the steam escape during cooking.

Bake the pie for about 45 minutes. Check by inserting a fine skewer into the chimney; it should slide into the potatoes easily. Transfer to a wire rack and carefully lift off the ring. Bring the cream to the boil in a pan and let bubble for 2–3 minutes, then season with salt and pepper. Pour it into the pie through the funnel a little at a time, allowing each addition to be absorbed (this will take about 20 minutes). Cut the warm pie at the table.

illustrated on previous page

serves 8

260g flan pastry (see page 23)
500g very firm medium button mushrooms,
   trimmed and wiped with a barely damp cloth
60g butter
salt and freshly ground pepper
250g podded fresh young peas
200ml double cream
30g mint leaves, chopped
1 egg
2 egg yolks

Roll out the pastry to a round, 3 mm thick, and use to line a 20 cm diameter (3.5 cm deep) flan ring (see pages 10–11). Chill for at least 20 minutes.

Preheat the oven to 190°C/Gas 5. Lightly prick the base of the pastry case. Bake the case blind, following the instructions on page 12, for 20 minutes. Remove the beans and paper and return the pastry case to the oven for 5 minutes. Set aside. Increase the oven setting to 200°C/Gas 6.

Halve or quarter the mushrooms, depending on size. Heat the butter in a frying pan and sauté the mushrooms for 4–5 minutes until they've released their liquid. Drain, season and leave to cool a little.

Cook the peas in simmering water for 2–3 minutes until barely tender. Drain, refresh in cold water and drain thoroughly, then tip into a bowl. Add the mushrooms and toss to mix.

Heat half the cream in a small saucepan. As soon as it comes to the boil, add the mint, take off the heat, cover and leave to infuse until almost cold. Whiz the cream in a blender for 1 minute, then pass through a fine chinois into a bowl. Using a whisk, gently fold in the rest of the cream, whole egg and egg yolks. Season with salt and pepper.

Put the mushrooms and peas into the pastry case and pour on the creamy mixture. Bake for 15 minutes, then lower the oven setting to 180°C/Gas 4 and cook for another 15 minutes. Test by gently inserting a knife tip into the flan; it should come out clean. Place on a wire rack and lift off the flan ring. Serve warm, cut into slices.

semi-confit cherry tomato tart

serves 6

260g pâte brisée (see pages 20–1)
4 tbsp white rice
salt and freshly ground pepper
6 tbsp strong Dijon mustard
2 tbsp double cream, lightly whipped
500g (about 36) semi-confit cherry tomatoes
   (see page 289)
6 basil leaves, snipped

Roll out the pastry to a round, 3mm thick, and use to line a 20cm diameter (3.5cm deep) flan ring (see pages 10–11). Chill for at least 20 minutes.

Preheat the oven to 190°C/Gas 5. Prick the base of the pastry case. Bake the case blind, following the instructions on page 12, for 40 minutes until it is completely cooked, removing the beans and paper and lowering the oven setting to 170°C/Gas 3 for the last 15 minutes. Lift off the flan ring, transfer the pastry case to a wire rack and leave to cool.

In the meantime, cook the rice in boiling salted water for 18 minutes. Refresh under cold running water and drain thoroughly. Tip the cooked rice into a bowl and mix with the mustard and then the whipped cream. Season and spread the rice mixture in the pastry case. Arrange the cherry tomatoes on the rice, placing those still with stalks in the centre.

Scatter over the snipped basil and serve at room temperature. Have some Guérande or Maldon salt and crushed pepper on the table to sprinkle on the tart.

The cherry tomatoes need to be lightly confit for this tart, in order to preserve their fresh fruity taste. To fully appreciate the flavour, serve at room temperature, never straight from the fridge.

illustrated on previous page

This lovely flan features pale, compact spear-shaped Belgian endive bulbs, also known as chicory, or simply endive in France. I like to serve it with a bowl of homemade beetroot crisps or a salad of lamb's lettuce with walnuts.

260g pâte brisée (see pages 20–1)
350g Belgian endive (chicory bulbs)
30g butter
50g tender celery leaves, finely snipped
juice of 1/2 lemon

600ml double cream
3 eggs
3 egg yolks
salt and freshly ground pepper
90g Roquefort, finely diced

Separate the endive leaves and cut into 1cm wide strips, about 6cm long. Melt the butter in a deep frying pan, then add the endive, celery leaves and lemon juice. Cook over a medium heat for about 10 minutes until the endive is about three-quarters cooked and still fairly firm. Tip into a colander to drain, cover with cling film and set aside to cool.

Roll out the pastry to a round, 2–3mm thick, and use to line a 20cm diameter (3.5cm deep) flan ring (see pages 10–11). Chill for at least 20 minutes.

Preheat the oven to 190°C/Gas 5. Prick the base of the pastry case. Bake blind, following the instructions on page 12, for 20 minutes. Remove the beans and paper and return to the oven for 5 minutes. Set aside. Increase the oven setting to 200°C/Gas 6.

In a bowl, mix the cream, eggs and egg yolks together with a whisk until just combined; don't overwork. Season to taste. Put the well-drained, still-warm endive mixture into a large bowl and stir in the Roquefort, then mix in the cream and egg mixture. Pour into the pastry case.

Bake for 15 minutes, then lower the oven setting to 180°C/Gas 4 and cook for another 15 minutes. To test, delicately insert a knife tip into the centre of the flamiche; if it comes out clean and smooth, the flan is ready. Transfer it to a wire rack and remove the flan ring. Serve the flamiche hot or warm, cut into slices.

serves 4

These simple croustades are full of the flavours of early summer – an ideal healthy lunch. Vary the vegetables according to the season and what you fancy. A salad of tender leaves is the perfect complement.

260g pâte brisée (see pages 20–1)
24 small asparagus spears or samphire sprigs
300g podded fresh young broad beans
80g butter

250g podded fresh young peas
1 shallot, about 80g, finely chopped
100ml medium dry white wine
24 baby spinach leaves

Roll out the pastry to a 2 – 3mm thickness. Using a 16cm cutter or plate as a guide, cut out 4 rounds. Use these to line 4 individual loose-bottomed quiche tins, 10cm in diameter and 3cm deep (see page 13). Leave to rest in the fridge for 20 minutes.

Preheat the oven to 180°C/Gas 4. Prick the pastry case bases. Bake the cases blind, following the instructions on page 13, for 10 minutes, then remove the beans and paper (or lining tins) and bake for another 5 minutes. Unmould onto a wire rack and leave to cool. Lower the oven setting to 120°C/Gas ½.

Blanch the asparagus or samphire for 1 minute, refresh in cold water, drain and set aside. Slip the broad beans out of their skins and put them into a small pan with 2 tbsp water and 30g butter. Cover and cook very gently for 1 minute. Add the peas and cook for another 2 minutes, or until the vegetables are tender but still have some bite. Transfer to a bowl using a slotted spoon.

Add the shallot to the cooking juices in the pan, then pour in the wine and let bubble to reduce by two-thirds. Whisk in the rest of the butter, a small piece at a time, then add the spinach and blanched asparagus or samphire and keep warm.

Warm the croustades in the low oven for 2 minutes. Add the peas and broad beans to the vegetables in the pan and heat gently for 2 minutes, stirring delicately. Divide the vegetables and cooking juices between the croustades and serve on warm plates.

lightly curried seafood flans

serves 6

375g pâte brisée (see pages 20–1)
24 fresh mussels, cleaned
75 ml dry white wine
1 shallot, finely chopped
3 large scallops
6 langoustines, cleaned
1 tbsp curry powder
100g tender green seaweed (optional)
75 ml double cream
1 whole egg
1 egg yolk
salt and freshly ground pepper

to serve
300g French beans, halved lengthways
3 tbsp groundnut oil
1 tbsp red wine vinegar

Put the mussels, wine and shallot in a large saucepan, cover tightly and cook briskly for 2–3 minutes until the mussels have opened; discard any that stay closed. Take them out of their shells and place in a bowl. Cover with cling film and set aside.

Pour the cooking juices into a small pan, heat to below simmering (no more than 80°C) and gently poach the scallops for 3 minutes. Remove with a slotted spoon and add to the mussels, leaving the juices in the pan.

Lightly cook the langoustines in simmering water for 2 minutes; drain. Pull off the heads from the langoustines, chop these and add them to the pan containing the reserved cooking juices. Sprinkle in the curry powder. Let bubble for 3–4 minutes, then strain through a chinois, pressing with the back of a spoon to extract as much juice as possible. You should have 4–5 tbsp; set aside. Keep the langoustine tails to one side.

Roll out the pastry to a 3 mm thickness. Using a 15 cm cutter or plate as a guide, cut out 6 rounds. Use these to line 6 individual flan tins, 10 cm in diameter and 2 cm deep (see page 13). Chill in the fridge for at least 20 minutes.

Preheat the oven to 180°C/Gas 4. Prick the pastry case bases. Bake the cases blind, following the instructions on page 13, for 10 minutes, then remove the beans and paper (or lining tins) and bake for another 5 minutes. Leave the cases in the tins; set aside.

illustrated on previous page

Tender seaweed is a tasty, attractive addition to these light, creamy seafood flans, but it is not always easy to obtain. If you can't find it, simply leave it out. Serve the flans straight from the oven to enjoy them at their best.

Halve the scallops horizontally and place one scallop disc in each flan case. Shell the langoustine tails, half them lengthways and place 2 halves around the scallop in each flan case. Fill up the gaps with the mussels. If using seaweed, arrange it on top.

In a bowl, mix the cream, egg, egg yolk and reserved curry-flavoured juices. Season with salt and pepper to taste. Pour the mixture over the seafood in the flan cases and bake for about 20 minutes until the filling has set. To check, delicately insert a knife tip into the centre; if it comes out clean the flans are done.

While the flans are in the oven, cook the French beans in boiling salted water until just tender. Drain and dress with the groundnut oil, wine vinegar and seasoning to taste.

As soon as the flans are ready, unmould them and place on warm individual plates. Arrange the beans alongside and serve at once.

croustades of salt cod brandade with fennel

serves 6

360g pâte brisée (see pages 20–1)
1 small fennel bulb, trimmed and cut
   into 3mm thick slices
salt and freshly ground pepper
200ml light olive oil
2 thyme sprigs
1 bay leaf
6 basil sprigs

brandade
350g salt cod, soaked in at least 2 changes
   of cold water for 24 hours
$^1/_2$ garlic clove, peeled
100ml extra virgin olive oil
100ml milk, boiled and slightly cooled
juice of $^1/_2$ lemon
12 green olives, pitted and chopped

First make the brandade. Drain the soaked salt cod, place in a small saucepan and cover with cold water. Bring to just below simmering and poach gently (at 80°C) for 8 minutes. Drain, then wrap in kitchen paper. Roll the garlic in fine salt, then rub it round the sides and base of a small heavy-based pan (preferably enamel) until it is gone.

Flake the cod into the garlicky pan. Using a spatula or your fingertips, crush the cod as you pour on half of the extra virgin olive oil in a thin stream (as if making mayonnaise).

Once the oil has all been absorbed, put the pan over an extremely low heat and pour in the warm milk in a thin stream to loosen the texture of the cod and make it creamy. Finish by pouring in the remaining oil and the lemon juice, then season to taste with pepper and salt if necessary (the cod is often salty enough). Keep warm.

Blanch the fennel slices in boiling salted water for 1 minute, then drain and pat dry. Heat the light olive oil in a pan until hot but not boiling. Add the fennel, thyme and bay leaf and cook over a medium heat for about 5 minutes. The fennel should be 'confit' – cooked but not fried. Leave it in the oil at room temperature.

Roll out the pastry to a 2–3mm thickness. Using a 14cm cutter or plate as a guide, cut out 6 rounds and use them to line 6 individual flan tins, 10cm in diameter and 1.5cm deep (see page 13). Chill in the fridge for at least 20 minutes.

Preheat the oven to 180°C/Gas 4. Prick the pastry case bases. Bake the cases blind, following the instructions on page 13, for 20 minutes. Remove the beans and paper (or lining tins)

and bake for another 5 minutes until fully cooked. Unmould and place on a wire rack.

Drain the fennel and place a slice in each croustade; the edges will come above the border. Mix the olives into the warm brandade and spoon over the fennel. Place on individual plates, garnish with basil and serve at once.

scrambled egg croustades with crab

serves 6

These exquisite croustades are perfect for a light lunch or Sunday brunch.

360g flan pastry (see page 23)
60g butter
9 eggs
salt and freshly ground pepper
180g white crab meat (ideally freshly prepared)
6 cooked small crab claws (optional)
60ml double cream
2 tbsp grainy mustard (preferably Meaux)

cucumber salad
1 medium cucumber
3 tbsp groundnut oil
juice of 2 lemons
few chives, snipped

Have ready 6 croustade or quiche tins, 10cm across the top and 1.5cm deep. Roll out the pastry to a 2–3mm thickness and, using a 14cm pastry cutter or plate as a guide, cut out 6 discs. Use these to line the tins (see page 13). Chill for 20 minutes.

Preheat the oven to 180°C/Gas 4. Prick the pastry case bases. Bake the cases blind, following the instructions on page 13, for 15 minutes, then remove the beans and paper (or lining tins) and bake for another 5 minutes until cooked.

Meanwhile, prepare the salad. Halve the cucumber lengthways, scoop out the seeds, then peel and cut into batons. Place in a bowl. Whisk the oil and lemon juice together, season lightly and pour over the cucumber batons. Toss to mix.

Unmould the croustades as soon as they are cooked and place on a wire rack. Place a deep frying pan over a low heat (using a heat diffuser mat if possible) and melt the butter. Break the eggs into a bowl, season and beat very lightly with a fork.

Pour the eggs into the pan and scramble gently, stirring almost continuously with a wooden spatula for about 3 minutes, or an extra minute or two if you like your eggs firmer. Meanwhile, warm the crab meat and claws if using in a steamer for 4–5 minutes. As soon as the scrambled eggs are ready, stir in the cream and take off the heat.

Divide the scrambled eggs between the pastry cases, top with the crab meat and dab with the mustard. Place the croustades on serving plates. Spoon the cucumber salad alongside and scatter with chives. If you like, place a crab claw on each plate. Serve at once.

240g pâte brisée (see pages 20–1)
2 medium apples (preferably Cox's)
140g butter
80g caster sugar
juice of ¹/₂ lemon
2 tbsp groundnut oil
2 boudins noirs (French black pudding),
    about 12 cm long
1 onion, about 160g, thinly sliced
salt and freshly ground pepper

Roll out the pastry to a round, 3mm thick, and use to line an 18cm diameter (2.5cm deep) flan ring (see pages 10–11). Chill for at least 20 minutes.

Preheat the oven to 190°C/Gas 5. Prick the base of the pastry case. Bake the case blind, following the instructions on page 12, for 40 minutes until it is completely cooked, removing the beans and paper for the last 15 minutes. Lift off the flan ring, put the tart on a wire rack and leave to cool. Lower the oven setting to 170°C/Gas 3.

Peel the apples, cut each one into 6 wedges and cut out the core and pips. Heat 60g of the butter in a frying pan, then add the apples with 60g of the sugar and the lemon juice. Cook over a medium heat for 10 minutes until the apples are golden. Transfer to a plate.

Heat another 20g butter and the rest of the sugar in the pan, add the onion and cook gently for 20 minutes. Right at the end, add 2 tbsp water. Tip into a bowl and set aside.

In another frying pan, heat the oil and remaining butter very gently, put in the boudins and heat them through for about 4 minutes without letting them colour, turning them every minute. Transfer to a plate.

Lightly spread the onion over the tart base. Cut each boudin into 4 thick slices and stand these upright on the onion. Arrange the apples in between. Heat the tart through in the oven for 10 minutes, then transfer to a board or plate. Serve immediately, with a salad of mixed leaves, as a starter or lunch.

cornish pasties

serves 6

My ex-head chef and friend Mark Dodson is a master at these pasties and used to serve them to our friends and family at the Waterside Inn. The classic pastry is made with lard, but I prefer to use pâte brisée.

460g pâte brisée (see pages 20–1)
450g lean braising beef
3 tbsp groundnut oil
300ml beef stock (good-quality ready-made
  is suitable)

1 onion, about 180g, thinly sliced
1 potato, about 180g, cut into 5mm dice
1 swede, about 180g, cut into 5mm dice
salt and freshly ground pepper
eggwash (1 egg yolk mixed with 1 tbsp milk)

To make the filling, cut the beef into 1.5cm cubes. Heat the oil in a deep frying pan and lightly sear the beef all over. Pour off the fat, then add the stock and cook gently for about an hour until the meat is meltingly tender. By now, the stock should have evaporated almost completely. If not, reduce over a medium heat. Tip the beef into a bowl and leave to cool.

Cook the onion, potato and swede separately in a little lightly salted water until just tender. Leave to cool in the cooking water, then drain and mix with the beef. The mixture shouldn't be too dry; if it is, add 2–3 tbsp of the cooking water. Cover with cling film and chill for several hours. (The filling can be made a day ahead.)

To assemble, roll out the pastry to a 2–3mm thickness. Using a 14cm cutter or plate as a guide, cut out 6 discs. Spoon the filling into an oval in the middle of each disc, and brush the borders of the pastry with eggwash. Fold up the sides of the pastry and bring them together to make a raised pasty, pinching hard with your fingertips in about a dozen places all along the crest to seal the pasty completely. Place on a baking sheet and brush with eggwash. Refrigerate for about 20 minutes.

Preheat the oven to 180°C/Gas 4. Bake the pasties for 25 minutes until deep golden; if necessary, increase the oven setting to 200°C/Gas 6 for the last 5 minutes. To enjoy the pasties at their best, serve at once.

makes about 30

720g flan pastry (see page 23)
150ml groundnut oil
450g lean braising beef, minced (through
  a medium blade)
300g onions, finely chopped
6 garlic cloves, finely chopped
300g tomatoes, peeled, deseeded and
  roughly chopped
$^1/_2$ tsp ground cumin
$^1/_2$ tsp dried oregano

$^1/_2$ tsp sweet paprika
600ml veal or beef stock (good
  ready-made is suitable)
1 tbsp fine salt
1 tbsp freshly ground pepper
300g Cheddar or Cantal, grated
150g cottage cheese
2 egg whites, lightly beaten
50g parsley, fried in groundnut oil,
  to finish (optional)

For the filling, heat half the oil in a frying pan. Add the minced beef and brown it over a high heat, then tip into a colander to drain off the fat.

Heat the remaining oil in a shallow saucepan over a medium heat, add the onions and sweat them for 5 minutes, then add the garlic and tomatoes and simmer for 20 minutes. Add the beef, cumin, oregano, paprika, stock, salt and pepper and cook gently for 30 minutes. Add the Cheddar and cottage cheese and bubble for 2–3 minutes. Tip into a bowl and leave to cool, then refrigerate until ready to use.

To assemble the empanadas, roll out about a fifth of the pastry to a 1.5–2mm thickness and cut out about 6 discs using a 9cm pastry cutter. Put a generous tablespoon (about 20g) of filling into the centre of the discs and brush the pastry edges with egg white. Fold the pastry over the filling to make turnovers and pinch the edges together between your thumb and index finger, giving the border a quarter-turn inwards towards the filling every 5mm to make a plaited edge and seal it completely. Repeat to use all the pastry and filling. Chill the empanadas for 20 minutes.

Preheat the oven to 180°C/Gas 4. Place the empanadas on a baking sheet and bake for 12–15 minutes until golden. Transfer to a wire rack.

Arrange the empanadas in a basket or on a platter and scatter with freshly fried parsley if you like. Serve hot.

apple tart

> This tart is truly delicious if it is eaten barely cool from the oven.
> Pâte brisée is more delicate, but flan pastry is easier to handle
> – the choice is yours.

**300g flan pastry (see page 23) or pâte brisée
   (see pages 20–1)
6 dessert apples, about 850g (ideally Cox's)
1 vanilla pod, split lengthways
60g butter
80g caster sugar**

Roll out the pastry to a round, 3mm thick, and use to line a lightly buttered 24cm
diameter (3mm deep) loose-bottomed tart tin or flan ring (see pages 10 – 11). Pinch
up the edges with your index finger and thumb at 1cm intervals to make a fluted edge
a little higher than the rim (see page 14). Chill in the fridge for at least 20 minutes.

Preheat the oven to 200°C/Gas 6. Peel, core and halve the apples. Place cut-side down on
a board and cut into 2mm thick slices. Put a third of the apples (the outer smaller slices)
into a saucepan. Keep the other two-thirds packed together (to stop them discolouring).
Add 50ml water, the vanilla pod and butter to the apples in the pan and cook gently until
tender. Take off the heat, discard the vanilla pod and work the apples, using a whisk, to
a compote consistency. Leave to cool. For the glaze, in a small pan, dissolve the sugar in
40ml water. Bring to the boil and bubble for 4 – 5 minutes to make a syrup. Leave to cool.

Prick the base of the pastry case lightly. Pour in the cold apple compote and spread
gently with a spoon. Arrange a border of overlapping apple slices around the tart, then
arrange another circle inside, with the slices facing the other way. Fill the centre with
a little rosette of small slices, trimming to fit as necessary. Bake for about 35 minutes
until the pastry and apples are evenly cooked to a light golden colour.

Leave the tart to cool for at least 20 minutes before removing the flan ring or tart tin.
Brush the top with the glaze, place the tart on a wire rack and leave until just cooled.
Transfer to a plate and serve cut into slices.

You'll come across versions of this sweet custard tart or *flan boulanger* in baker's shops all over France. It brings back memories of my childhood. Now when I make it, I like to serve it with lightly poached prunes and candied orange peel.

sweet custard tart with poached prunes

serves 6

260g flan pastry (see page 23)
5 egg yolks
100g caster sugar
20g plain flour
15g custard powder
400ml milk
1 vanilla pod, split lengthways

to serve
16 prunes (preferably Agen), pitted
150g caster sugar
100g candied orange peel sticks
(see page 291), optional

Roll out the pastry to a round, 3mm thick, and use to line a 20cm diameter (3.5cm deep) flan ring (see pages 10–11). Crimp the pastry border with your index finger and thumb (see page 14). Chill for at least 20 minutes.

Preheat the oven to 190°C/Gas 5. Prick the base of the pastry case. Bake the case blind, following the instructions on page 12, for 15 minutes. Set aside. Increase the oven setting to 200°C/Gas 6.

Meanwhile, for the filling, whisk the egg yolks with one-third of the sugar in a bowl. Add the flour and custard powder and whisk thoroughly.

Heat the milk with the rest of the sugar and the vanilla pod in a heavy-based pan. As soon as it comes to the boil, pour onto the egg yolk mixture, stirring well, then return to the pan. Bring to the boil over a medium heat, stirring continuously with the whisk. Allow the custard to bubble, still stirring, for 2 minutes. Remove the vanilla pod.

Spread the hot custard in the flan case and bake for 25 minutes or until lightly golden on the surface. Carefully slide on a wire rack, lift off the ring and leave to cool completely.

For the prunes, dissolve the sugar in 150ml water in a pan over a medium heat. Add the prunes and poach gently for 2–6 minutes, depending on size and softness, until tender.

Serve the tart with the poached prunes and candied orange peel if you like.

illustrated on previous page

serves 8

Everyone loves this classic pie with its tangy lemon cream filling
and soft, billowy meringue topping.

240g pâte brisée (see pages 20–1)
eggwash (1 egg yolk mixed with 1 tbsp milk)

lemon cream
8 lemons
75g cornflour
225g caster sugar

100g butter
6 egg yolks
icing sugar, to dust

meringue topping
4 egg whites
100g caster sugar

For the lemon cream, grate the zest from 4 lemons, then squeeze the juice from all of them and combine with the grated zest and 35 ml water. Put the cornflour in a bowl and pour on a third of the lemon mixture, whisking until smooth. Heat the remaining lemon mixture in a pan with the sugar and butter until smooth, then bring to the boil. Pour onto the cornflour mix, whisking, then return to the pan. Still whisking, bring to the boil and boil for 2–3 minutes. Take off the heat and whisk in the egg yolks, then pass through a muslin-lined chinois into a bowl. Dust the surface with icing sugar and leave to cool.

Roll out the pastry to a round, 2–3 mm thick. Use to line a lightly greased, loose-bottomed 18 cm diameter (2.5 cm deep) flan tin (see pages 10–11). Chill for 20 minutes.

Preheat the oven to 190°C / Gas 5. Prick the pastry base. Bake the case blind for 35 minutes (see page 12). Remove beans and paper. Brush the inside with eggwash; return to the oven for 3 minutes. Unmould and place on a wire rack. Lower the oven setting to 150°C / Gas 2.

To make the meringue, beat the egg whites in a clean bowl with a balloon whisk or electric beater to soft peaks, then little by little, whisk in the sugar. Continue to beat for 5 minutes until the meringue is stiff and glossy. Put into a piping bag fitted with a large fluted nozzle.

Put the pastry case on a baking sheet and fill with lemon cream, spreading it carefully. Pipe the meringue evenly over the top. Cook in the oven for 45–50 minutes until the meringue feels a little crunchy to the touch. Leave to cool for 30 minutes or so. This pie is best served at room temperature.

greengage tart

serves 6

260g flan pastry (see page 23)
400g crème pâtissière (see page 292)
400g very ripe greengages (about 15),
   halved and pitted
30g caster sugar

Roll out the pastry to a round, 3 mm thick, and use to line a 20 cm diameter (3.5 cm deep) flan ring (see pages 10–11). Crimp the pastry border with your index finger and thumb (see page 14). Chill for at least 20 minutes.

Preheat the oven to 190°C/Gas 5. Prick the base of the pastry case. Use a spoon to spread the crème pâtissière evenly in the case. Arrange the greengage halves rounded side-up on top. Bake for 30 minutes, then remove the tart from the oven and increase the oven setting to 200°C/Gas 6.

Sprinkle the tart with caster sugar and return it to the hot oven for another 10 minutes until the sugar has partially dissolved and lightly caramelised. Lift off the flan ring and slide the tart onto a wire rack. Leave to cool slightly, or completely if you prefer.

Serve the tart warm or at room temperature.

You can use other types of plum for this tart, such as purple quetsches, mirabelles or Victoria plums… greengages just happen to be my favourite. If they are not fully ripe, poach in a light sugar syrup for 5–10 minutes until tender and drain well before arranging on the tart.

serves 6

240g pâte brisée (see pages 20–1)
10g crushed white peppercorns
300g ricotta cheese
100g clear honey
75g shelled pistachio nuts, blanched
    and skinned
1 lemon, cut into wedges (optional)

Roll out the pastry to a round, 3mm thick, and use to line an 18cm diameter (2.5cm deep) flan ring (see pages 10–11). Chill for at least 20 minutes.

Preheat the oven to 190°C/Gas 5. Prick the base of the pastry case. Bake the case blind, following the instructions on page 12, for 40 minutes until it is completely cooked, removing the beans and paper and lowering the oven setting to 170°C/Gas 3 for the last 15 minutes. Lift off the flan ring, slide the tart onto a wire rack and leave to cool.

Using a fork, mix the crushed pepper delicately into the ricotta. Drizzle half of the honey over the base of the tart case from a warm spoon, then spread the ricotta evenly over the base, without packing it down. Scatter the pistachios over the surface and finally drizzle over the rest of the honey. Serve at once, with lemon wedges for squeezing if you like.

This rustic tart is so simple, yet so divine. When fresh figs are in season, serve some perfectly ripe ones on the side, along with lemon wedges. Squeezing a few drops of lemon juice onto the tart lifts the flavour.

cherry clafoutis

serves 6

240g pâte brisée (pages 20–1)
1 egg
40g plain flour
40g butter, melted and cooled slightly
1 tbsp kirsch (optional)

30g caster sugar
75ml cold milk
1 vanilla pod, split lengthways
450g very ripe black cherries, pitted
icing sugar, to dust

Break the egg into a bowl, add the flour and mix using a whisk, without overworking. Add the melted butter and kirsch if using, then gradually work in the caster sugar and milk. Scrape the vanilla seeds from the pod with the tip of a knife and stir into the mixture.

Roll out the pastry to a round, 3 mm thick, and use to line an 18 cm diameter (2.5 cm deep) flan ring (see pages 10–11). Chill for at least 20 minutes.

Preheat the oven to 170°C/Gas 3. Prick the base of the pastry case. Bake the case blind, following the instructions on page 12, for 15 minutes. Remove the beans and paper, turn the oven up to 180°C/Gas 4 and bake for another 5 minutes. Remove from the oven.

Turn the oven setting to 200°C/Gas 6. Spread the cherries evenly in the pastry case, then pour in the batter to come just up to the rim. Bake in the hot oven for about 25 minutes until the surface is a light hazelnut brown colour. Check by gently inserting a knife tip in the centre; if it comes out clean, the clafoutis is done. Slide onto a wire rack and lift off the flan ring.

Transfer the clafoutis to a serving plate, dust generously with icing sugar and serve warm.

This traditional French pudding is a lovely way to serve soft stone fruit – try it also with apricots, mirabelles and greengages. A splash of kirsch enhances the flavour of the fruit.

This tart is inexpensive, easy to make and always popular. It also fills the kitchen with an enticing aroma as it cooks. A dollop of crème fraîche is the perfect complement.

340g flan pastry (see page 23)
finely pared zest of 1 orange, cut into pieces
300g peeled and deseeded pumpkin
100g butter
180g caster sugar
50g shelled almonds, skinned and toasted
eggwash (1 egg yolk mixed with 1 tbsp milk)

Warm the oven to its lowest setting (about 50°C). Lay the pieces of orange zest on a baking sheet and dry in the oven for about 2 hours. Leave to cool.

Cut the pumpkin into 2 cm cubes and steam for 10–15 minutes until half-cooked. Remove from the steamer. Heat the butter in a frying pan and add the pumpkin and 120g of the sugar. Cook over a medium heat for 6–7 minutes, then tip into a bowl and set aside to cool.

Put the almonds, orange zest and the rest of the sugar in a small food processor and blitz for 1 minute to chop into small pieces.

Roll out 260g of the pastry to a round, 2 mm thick. Use to line a loose-bottomed 20 cm diameter (2.5 cm deep) flan tin (see pages 10–11). Crimp the pastry between your thumb and index finger every 5 mm to make an attractive serrated border (see page 14). Chill for at least 20 minutes.

Preheat the oven to 180°C / Gas 4. Prick the base of the pastry case, then spread the pumpkin cubes evenly in the case. Roll out the remaining pastry to a 20 cm long band and cut into 5 mm wide strips. Arrange these in a lattice over the pumpkin (as shown). Lightly brush the pastry strips with eggwash.

Bake the tart for 40 minutes until golden. If necessary, increase the oven setting to 200°C / Gas 6 for the last 5 minutes to deepen the colour of the pastry. Unmould the tart immediately and place on a wire rack. Sprinkle the exposed pumpkin with the almond and orange mixture and serve.

baked apples in a pastry cage

serves 4

Enveloped in crisp sugar-glazed pastry is an impressive way to serve baked apples. Accompany with crème anglaise (see page 242).

520g pâte brisée (see pages 20–1)
8 dates, pitted and diced
50ml very fragrant jasmine tea
4 medium crisp apples (preferably Cox's),
    about 700g
30g caster sugar, to dust

Put the dates in a bowl, pour the tea over them and leave to infuse for 10 minutes. Prise out the core from each apple, using an apple corer, and prick the skin in several places with the tip of a knife. Fill the cavities with the dates.

Preheat the oven to 160°C/Gas 2¹/₂. Roll out a quarter of the pastry to a 22cm diameter disc, 2mm thick. Cut a 2cm hole in the centre using a pastry cutter. Starting 1.5cm from the hole, use the tip of a small sharp knife to make a series of 4cm long incisions in the pastry, 1cm apart, radiating out from the hole. Now make short 1.5cm cuts inwards from the outer edge at 1.5cm intervals to make a serrated border.

Brush an apple with water, then immediately lift the pastry disc with a palette knife and place it over the apple. Brush a little water over the base of the apple, gather the edges of the pastry underneath and press together with your fingertips to seal it. Put the 'caged' apple on a baking sheet and prepare the others in the same way. Bake in the oven for about 1¹/₂ hours, checking with a knife tip that the apples are cooked; it should slide in with no resistance.

Remove the apples from the oven, dust with the sugar and glaze with a cook's blowtorch, or place under a very hot grill until the sugar begins to melt on the pastry. Serve the apples on individual plates, if not immediately, within half an hour.

serves 8

240g pâte brisée (see pages 20–1)
500g gooseberries, either fresh or bottled
   in syrup (drained weight 400g)
1 litre sugar syrup (see page 291), if using
   fresh gooseberries
250g crème pâtissière (see page 292),
   flavoured with 3 star anise instead of vanilla
finely grated zest of 2 lemons

meringue topping
4 egg whites
100g caster sugar

Roll out the pastry to a round, 3mm thick. Use to line a lightly greased, loose-bottomed 18cm diameter (2.5cm deep) flan tin (see pages 10–11). Chill for at least 20 minutes.

Preheat the oven to 190°C/Gas 5. Prick the base of the pastry case. Bake the case blind, following the instructions on page 12, for 35 minutes. Remove the beans and paper and return the pastry case to the oven for 5 minutes. Remove the flan tin and slide the pastry case off its base onto a wire rack. Lower the oven setting to 150°C/Gas 2.

If using fresh gooseberries, gently poach them in the sugar syrup below simmering (at 80°C) for 5–10 minutes, depending on their ripeness. Leave them to cool in the syrup.

To make the meringue, beat the egg whites in a clean bowl with a balloon whisk or electric beater until they form peaks, then little by little, whisk in the sugar. Continue to beat for 5 minutes until the meringue is stiff and glossy. Put into a piping bag fitted with a large fluted nozzle.

Place the pastry case on a baking sheet and half-fill with the star anise infused crème pâtissière. Drain the fresh or bottled gooseberries thoroughly of their syrup, and roll them in the grated lemon zests. Arrange evenly on the crème pâtissière. Pipe the meringue generously and evenly over the berries. Cook in the oven for 45–50 minutes until the meringue is slightly crunchy.

Leave to cool for at least 30 minutes. Serve the pie at room temperature, using a very sharp knife to cut it into portions.

Pâte sucrée and pâte sablée both contain a high proportion of sugar and butter, making them delicate and crumbly on the palate, particularly pâte sablée. In a professional kitchen, type 45 flour, often called pastry flour, is generally used to make these doughs, though type 55 (bread flour) may be substituted for a less fragile pastry. The pastries are best eaten soon after they are cooked, although they can be kept in a dry airtight container for a few days. Both pastries are a perfect match for all fruits, especially soft berries, and they make a wonderful crumbly base for my orange cheesecake. These are the first pastries I taught my grandchildren to make. They quickly learnt the secret of producing perfect little tartlets and sablés in all sorts of original shapes and forms, and could hardly wait until they were cooked to devour them. A real source of pride for me and pleasure for them!

enriched
sweet pastries

pâte sucrée

makes about 520g

This sweet pastry is mostly used for fruit tarts. It is easier to work with than *pâte sablée* (overleaf) and, once cooked, *pâte sucrée* pastry cases are less fragile. The dough can be made in advance and kept well wrapped in the fridge for several days, or frozen for up to 3 months.

250g plain flour
100g butter, cubed and slightly softened
100g icing sugar, sifted
pinch of salt
2 eggs, at room temperature

Put the flour in a mound on a work surface (ideally marble) and make a well. Put in the butter, icing sugar and salt, and mix these ingredients together with your fingertips.

Gradually draw the flour into the centre and mix with your fingertips until the dough becomes slightly grainy.

When the dough is well amalgamated, knead it a few times with the palm of your hand until smooth. Roll the dough into a ball, wrap in cling film, and rest in the fridge for 1–2 hours before using.

Again, make a well and add the eggs. Work them into the flour mixture, using your fingertips, until the dough begins to hold together.

When the dough is rested and you are ready to use it, unwrap and roll out on a lightly floured clean surface to a 2–3mm thickness.

pâte sablée makes about 650g

Pâte sablée is more fragile and delicate to work with than *pâte sucrée*, but it melts in the mouth like no other pastry. If well wrapped, it will keep perfectly in the fridge for up to a week, or in the freezer for up to 3 months.

250g plain flour
200g butter, cut into small pieces and
   slightly softened
100g icing sugar, sifted
pinch of salt
2 egg yolks

Heap the flour on the work surface and make a well. Put in the butter, icing sugar and salt. With your fingertips, mix and cream the butter with the sugar and salt, then add the egg yolks and work them in delicately with your fingertips.

Little by little, draw the flour into the centre and work the mixture delicately with your fingers until you have a homogeneous dough.

Using the palm of your hand, push the dough away from you 3 or 4 times until it is completely smooth. Roll it into a ball, wrap in cling film and refrigerate until ready to use.

These enriched sweet pastries are both suitable for making little pastry cases that lend themselves to all kinds of simple fillings – fresh fruit, lemon curd, chocolate mousse, even ice cream. Fill the tartlets just before serving so that the pastry doesn't go soggy.

Tartlet cases Have ready 4 tartlet tins, 10 cm diameter (2 cm deep). Roll out 200g of either pastry on a lightly floured surface to a 2 mm thickness and cut out 4 rounds, using a 14 cm cutter or plate as a guide. Place the pastry rounds in the tartlet tins and use your thumbs to ease the pastry in, to line the tins (see page 13). Rest in the fridge for at least 20 minutes.

Preheat the oven to 180°C/Gas 4. Prick the bottom of the pastry cases in 2 or 3 places with a fork. Bake blind, following the instructions on page 13, for 10 minutes, then remove the beans and paper (or lining tins) and bake for another 5 minutes. Unmould the cases onto a wire rack and leave to cool. Fill once cold, or store in an airtight container – the tartlet cases will keep well for a few days.

Fruit tartlets Fill the pastry cases with chantilly cream (see page 295) flavoured with a touch of vanilla or some passion fruit seeds if you like, or crème pâtissière (see page 292). Pile your chosen ripe fruits on top – raspberries, strawberries, blueberries, sliced peaches – the choice is yours. Just don't pack the fruit in too tightly. Top each tartlet with a sprig of mint and serve immediately.

Ice cream tartlets Make tartlet cases as above (or shallow square cases or barquettes if you prefer, using suitable moulds). Bake and cool as above. Fill with a ball of ice cream or sorbet and serve at once.

lemon tart

serves 8

This classic tart tastes even better if you make it in advance.
I like to caramelise the surface using a cook's blowtorch, but you
can simply dust it with icing sugar if you prefer.

280g pâte sucrée (see pages 74–5)
eggwash (1 egg yolk mixed with 1 tbsp milk)
5 unwaxed lemons, washed
9 eggs
375g caster sugar
300ml double cream, lightly whipped
30g icing sugar, to glaze

Roll out the pastry to a round, 3mm thick, and use to line a lightly greased 20cm diameter (4cm deep) flan ring (see pages 10–11). Chill for at least 20 minutes.

Preheat the oven to 180°C/Gas 4. Prick the pastry base lightly. Bake the pastry case blind, following the instructions on page 12, for 20 minutes. Remove the beans and paper and cook the pastry case for another 15 minutes. Lower the oven setting to 170°C/Gas 3. Let the pastry case cool slightly, then brush the inside with eggwash and return to the oven for 5 minutes.

For the filling, finely grate the zest from the lemons and set aside, then squeeze the juice and strain through a chinois to eliminate the pulp and pips. Combine the eggs and sugar together in a bowl, stirring with a whisk until thoroughly amalgamated. Pour on the lemon juice and add the zest, stirring as you go. Finally, delicately fold in the whipped cream; do not overwork the mixture. Cover and chill for about 30 minutes.

To cook the lemon tart, heat the oven to 150°C/Gas 2. Lightly beat the cold lemon cream with a spatula, pour into the pastry case and bake immediately for 1 hour 20 minutes. Leave to cool and firm up for a while before removing the ring (but do so while the tart is still slightly warm). Set aside until cold. (You can prepare the tart up to 24 hours ahead.)

Just before serving, dust the surface with half of the icing sugar and caramelise it with a cook's blowtorch. Repeat with the remaining icing sugar and serve immediately. Cut the tart carefully using a sharp knife, as the caramelised surface is very delicate.

The flavours of orange and rhubarb work well together and the crème pâtissière counteracts their acidity perfectly. Don't fill the tartlet cases too soon before serving, or the syrupy rhubarb will soften the pastry.

220g pâte sucrée (see pages 74–5)
400g tender young rhubarb
140g caster sugar
1 large juicy orange
40g butter
120g crème pâtissière (see page 292)

Roll out the pastry to a 3mm thickness. Using a 12cm cutter or plate as a guide, cut out 6 rounds. Use these to line 6 tartlet tins, 6cm in diameter and 3cm deep (see page 13). Cut off the excess pastry with a sharp knife. Rest the tartlet cases in the fridge for 20 minutes.

Preheat the oven to 180°C/Gas 4. Prick the base of each pastry case lightly and bake blind (see page 13), for 15 minutes. Remove the beans and paper (or lining tins) and return to the oven for 5 minutes. Leave in the tins for 5 minutes, then unmould onto a wire rack.

Peel away any stringy bits from the rhubarb, halve the stalks lengthways if large, then cut into 2cm lengths. Place in a saucepan and barely cover with water. Add 100g of the sugar and heat to dissolve, then bring to the boil. Lower the heat and simmer for 5 minutes, then leave to stand for 10 minutes. Drain the rhubarb well, reserving the liquor. Return the liquor to the pan and boil to reduce until thick and syrupy.

Peel the orange with a flexible knife, removing all the white pith. Slide the knife blade between each segment to release it from the membrane, then cut the segments in half. Heat the butter in a frying pan, sprinkle on the remaining 40g sugar and cook for a few minutes, stirring with a wooden spoon to make a light caramel. Add the rhubarb and glaze it in the caramel for 2–3 minutes, then add the orange segments and finally the reduced poaching syrup. Simmer for 2 minutes, then tip into a bowl and leave to cool.

Just before serving, divide the crème pâtissière between the tartlet cases and pile the rhubarb and oranges on top.

chocolate and raspberry tart

serves 8

240g pâte sucrée (see pages 74–5)
250g raspberries
20g mint leaves, finely snipped

chocolate ganache
250ml whipping cream
200g good-quality dark chocolate, 60–70% cocoa solids (preferably Valrhona), finely chopped
25g liquid glucose
50g butter, cut into small pieces

Roll out the pastry to a round, 2mm thick, and use to line a lightly greased 20cm diameter (2.5cm deep) flan ring (see pages 10–11). Chill for at least 20 minutes.

Preheat the oven to 190°C/Gas 5. Prick the base of the pastry case. Bake the case blind, following the instructions on page 12, for 20 minutes. Lower the oven setting to 180°C/Gas 4, remove the beans and paper and bake the pastry case for another 5 minutes.

Place on a wire rack, lift off the ring and leave the tart case until cold. Set aside 24 of the best raspberries. Halve the rest, delicately mix with the snipped mint and spread evenly in the pastry case.

For the chocolate ganache, bring the cream to the boil in a heavy-based pan over a medium heat. Take off the heat, add the chocolate and glucose, and mix with a whisk to a very smooth cream. Still whisking, incorporate the butter, a piece at a time.

Pour the ganache over the halved raspberries to fill the pastry case. Set aside until cold, then chill the tart for at least 2 hours before serving.

Use a very sharp knife dipped in very hot water and wiped dry to cut each slice. Place the tart slices on individual plates with the reserved raspberries. Serve cold, but not straight from the fridge.

serves 6

220g pâte sucrée (see pages 74–5)
750g very ripe, fragrant strawberries
300g chantilly cream (see page 295)
150g crème pâtissière (see page 292)
a few mint sprigs
icing sugar, to dust

Roll out the pastry to a round, 2–3 mm thick, and use to line an 18 cm diameter (2.5 cm deep) flan ring (see pages 10–11). Chill for at least 20 minutes.

Preheat the oven to 190°C/Gas 5. Prick the base of the pastry case. Bake the case blind, following the instructions on page 12, for 40 minutes until it is fully cooked, removing the beans and paper for the last 15 minutes. Lift off the flan ring, transfer the pastry case to a wire rack and leave to cool.

Halve the strawberries if they are large; otherwise leave them whole. Delicately fold the chantilly cream into the crème pâtissière and fill the pastry case with this mixture. Arrange the strawberries on top, heaping them up slightly in the centre.

Slide the tart onto a serving plate, decorate with mint sprigs and dust lightly with icing sugar to serve.

For this tart filling, the crème pâtissière should be strongly flavoured with vanilla or, better still, the grated zest of 2 oranges. Assemble the tart just before serving to enjoy it at its best.

apricot tart

serves 6

This vibrant tart is a lovely way to enjoy fresh apricots during their short season; at other times you can use tinned fruit.

220g pâte sucrée (see pages 74–5)
350g crème pâtissière (see page 292)
8 very ripe apricots, halved and stoned, or
   tinned apricot halves in syrup
80g caster sugar

Roll out the pastry to a round, 2–3 mm thick, and use to line an 18 cm diameter (2.5 cm deep) flan ring (see pages 10–11). Chill for at least 20 minutes.

Preheat the oven to 190°C/Gas 5. Prick the base of the pastry case. Bake the case blind, following the instructions on page 12, for 20 minutes. Remove the beans and paper and bake the pastry case for another 5 minutes, then set aside to cool. Increase the oven setting to 200°C/Gas 6.

Use a spoon to spread the crème pâtissière evenly in the pastry case. Arrange 12 apricot halves around the edge, rounded side-up and overlapping slightly, and place a good apricot half in the centre of the tart. Cut the remaining apricot halves in two and arrange them, standing upright, all round the central apricot like flower petals. Bake the tart in the hot oven for 20 minutes.

Meanwhile, put 80 ml water in a small saucepan, add the sugar and heat to dissolve, then bring to the boil. Let bubble for 5 minutes to make a syrupy glaze.

When the tart is ready, transfer it to a wire rack and lift off the flan ring. Let it cool for a minute or two, then brush generously with the syrup to glaze.

Raising the apricot 'petals' on the tart ensures that their tips become lightly caramelised, which looks effective and adds a hint of dark caramel flavour.

I must have tasted hundreds of cheesecakes in the course of my career, but I've never found one as good as this!

orange cheesecake

serves 8

280g pâte sablée (see page 76)
4 oranges
350g fromage frais or cream cheese
350g curd cheese
150g soured cream
175g caster sugar
4 eggs

to finish
6 tbsp low-sugar Seville orange marmalade,
 barely warmed and strained
candied orange peel sticks from 2 oranges
 (see page 291), optional

Roll out the pastry to a round, 3 mm thick, and use to line a lightly greased 20 cm diameter (4 cm deep) flan ring (see pages 10–11). Chill for at least 20 minutes.

Preheat the oven to 170°C/Gas 3. Prick the base of the pastry case. Bake the case blind, following the instructions on page 12, for 30 minutes. Remove the beans and paper and return to the oven for 5 minutes, then set aside to cool. Lower the oven setting to 140°C/Gas 1.

For the filling, finely grate the zest from the oranges, then squeeze the juice and strain through a chinois. Put the soft cheeses, soured cream and sugar in a large bowl and mix thoroughly with a spatula. In another bowl, whisk the eggs until frothy, then delicately incorporate them into the cheese mixture. Add the orange zest and juice and mix with the spatula until evenly combined.

Pour the filling into the pastry case and bake in the low oven for 1 1/2 hours. To check that the cheesecake is cooked, insert a fine skewer into the centre; it should come out clean. Place on a wire rack and leave for about 20 minutes before removing the flan ring. Let cool completely, then place in the least cool part of your fridge until ready to serve.

To serve, carefully spread an even layer of marmalade over the surface of the cheesecake. Wait a few minutes for the glaze to set, then cut the cheesecake into portions using a very sharp knife. Serve on individual plates, with confit orange peel sticks, drizzled with a little of their syrup, on the side if you like.

illustrated on previous page

serves 8

I adore this luxurious Spanish custard tart. If you happen to be in the Barcelona region, try the Catalan tart at le Mas de Torrent Relais et Châteaux – it is simply the best.

220g pâte sablée (see page 76)
800ml full-fat (cow's) milk
200ml goat's milk
1/2 cinnamon stick, broken into pieces
finely pared zest of 1 orange

finely pared zest of 1 lemon
200g caster sugar
8 egg yolks
40g cornflour
30g icing sugar, sifted, to dust

Roll out the pastry to a round, 2–3mm thick, and use to line a lightly greased 20cm diameter (1.5cm deep) flan ring (see pages 10–11). Chill for at least 20 minutes.

Preheat the oven to 190°C/Gas 5. Prick the base of the pastry case. Bake the case blind, following the instructions on page 12, for 20 minutes. Lower the oven setting to 170°C/Gas 3. Remove the beans and paper and return the pastry case to the oven for 10 minutes. Leave to cool, lifting off the flan ring before the pastry is completely cold.

For the Catalan cream, pour the cow's and goat's milk into a saucepan, add the cinnamon, citrus zests and two-thirds of the sugar and slowly bring to the boil. Meanwhile, whisk the egg yolks in a bowl with the rest of the sugar to a light foam, then whisk in the cornflour until smooth. As the milk comes to the boil, strain it through a chinois onto the egg mixture, whisking continuously.

Pour the Catalan cream into the pastry case and spread it evenly with a palette knife. (If you have any cream left over, pour it into one or two small crème brûlée dishes and eat it as a treat as soon as it has cooled.)

When the cream in the pastry case is cold and you are ready to serve the tart, dust the surface with icing sugar and glaze with a searingly hot salamander or a cook's blowtorch until very lightly caramelised. Use a very sharp knife to cut the tart and serve at once.

serves 8

240g pâte sablée (see page 76)
230g butter, softened
80g maple syrup
150g caster sugar
3 eggs
330g shelled pecan nuts
50g plain flour

Roll out the pastry to a round, 3 mm thick, and use it to line a lightly greased 20 cm diameter (2.5 cm deep) flan ring (see pages 10 – 11). Chill for at least 20 minutes.

Preheat the oven to 180°C / Gas 4. Prick the base of the pastry case. Bake the case blind, following the instructions on page 12, for 20 minutes. Remove the beans and paper and return the pastry case to the oven for 5 minutes. Unmould and place on a wire rack. Lower the oven setting to 170°C / Gas 3.

For the filling, work the butter, maple syrup and sugar together in a bowl using a whisk until creamy. Incorporate the eggs one at a time, working each one in with the whisk before adding the next.

Set aside about 100g of the best pecan halves; coarsely chop the rest. Mix the chopped pecans and the flour into the filling, taking care not to overwork the mixture.

Pour the filling into the cooked pastry case. Arrange the pecan halves on top and bake in the oven for 20 – 25 minutes until the surface is golden brown and the top feels firm to the touch.

Lift off the flan ring and leave the pie to cool until warm before slicing and serving.

This soft-textured American-style pie is best served warm with vanilla ice cream. If left until cold, the tart loses some of its flavour.

pear clafoutis

serves 8

This heavenly comfort pudding is best served warm with a spoonful of crème fraîche, or a scoop of chocolate ice cream on the side.

220g pâte sablée (see page 76)
4 ripe pears
juice of 1 lemon
1 litre sugar syrup (see page 291)
120 ml milk

120 ml double cream
1 vanilla pod, split lengthways
175g caster sugar, plus extra to sprinkle
4 eggs
20g plain flour

Peel the pears with a vegetable peeler, leaving a deep collar of skin around the stalk of one of them. Brush the pears with lemon juice. Leave the one with the collar whole. Halve the others and scoop out the cores with a melon baller or knife. Put all the pears in a saucepan with the sugar syrup and bring to a simmer, then lower the heat and poach gently (at about 90°C) for 20 minutes until tender, depending on ripeness. Leave to cool in the syrup.

Heat the milk, cream, vanilla pod and two-thirds of the sugar in a saucepan. In a bowl, lightly whisk the eggs and remaining sugar, then add the flour. As the creamy milk comes to the boil, pour it onto the eggs, whisking well. Leave until cold, stirring occasionally.

Roll out the pastry to a round, 3mm thick. Use to line a lightly greased 18cm diameter (2.5cm deep) loose-bottomed tart tin (see pages 10–11). Chill for 20 minutes. Preheat the oven to 190°C/Gas 5. Prick the pastry base. Bake blind, following the instructions on page 12, for 15 minutes. Remove beans and paper and return to the oven for 5 minutes.

To assemble, drain the pears and pat dry. From the base, cut the pear halves two-thirds of the way up into 2mm thick slices. Cut the whole pear just below the collar and place the top in the centre of the pastry case; dice the rest of the pear and place in the case. Lay the sliced pear halves on top, with their rounded ends outwards, and fan them out slightly.

Discard the vanilla and pour the clafoutis batter over the pears. Immediately bake for 30 minutes until cooked and golden. Place on a wire rack and leave to cool for 20 minutes, then unmould and sprinkle generously with caster sugar. Serve at once, while still warm.

The mincemeat needs to macerate for at least 2 weeks before using, so make it well in advance. You'll have more than you need for one batch of pies; save the rest for the following year when it will taste even better. Make the little mince pies just a few days before Christmas and keep in a dry place. Allow three per person, as each one is only a delicious mouthful.

makes 48 mince pies (2.5.kg mincemeat)

360g pâte sablée (see page 76)
eggwash (1 egg yolk mixed with 1 tbsp milk)
60g caster sugar

mincemeat
225g sultanas
450g raisins
450g currants
450g beef fat, finely minced, or suet
1 large cooking apple, peeled, cored
   and grated

100g glacé fruits (cherries, orange and
   angelica), finely chopped
350g soft brown sugar
1 tsp freshly grated nutmeg
1 tsp freshly grated mace
1 tsp ground cloves
1 tsp ground cinnamon
50ml Cognac or rum
grated zest and juice of 1 lemon

For the mincemeat, rinse the dried fruit, dry thoroughly and roughly chop the sultanas and raisins. Put the beef fat or suet in a very large bowl, then add the dried fruit and all the other ingredients in the order listed, mixing with a spatula until well combined. Cover with cling film and leave to macerate in a cool larder or the vegetable drawer of the fridge for 24 hours. Pack the mincemeat into sterilised preserving or kilner jars. Make sure there are no air pockets by pushing the mixture hard into the bottom of the jars and filling them to the brim. Cover each with a waxed paper disc and seal the jars with the clip. Store them in a larder or the vegetable drawer of the fridge.

To make the mince pies, roll out the pastry to a 2mm thickness and use 6cm and 4.5cm pastry cutters to cut out 48 discs of each size. Line 48 lightly greased 4.5cm diameter (1cm deep) mini tartlet tins with the larger discs, prick the bases and fill with mincemeat. (Alternatively, make them in 4 batches.)

Lightly brush the borders of the smaller discs with cold water and place them on top of the filled mince pies. Press the edges gently to ensure that the lids are sealed to the pastry cases. Leave to rest in the fridge for 20 minutes.

Preheat the oven to 180°C/Gas 4. Brush the pastry with eggwash and bake the pies for about 10 minutes until pale golden brown. Sprinkle with the caster sugar and return to the oven for 1 minute to glaze. Immediately unmould the pies before they cool in the tin, and place on a wire rack. Serve warm, with a glass of sherry or a cup of coffee.

medley of mini sablés

makes about 30

These little sablés are delicious served with coffee or at teatime.

550g pâte sablée (see page 76)
eggwash (1 egg yolk mixed with 1 tbsp milk)

toppings
4 tbsp raspberry jam
20 flaked almonds
1 tbsp instant coffee
1 tbsp apricot jam
75g chantilly cream (see page 295)
12 bilberries or small blueberries
6 small clusters of redcurrants
icing sugar, to dust

Roll out 450g of the pâte sablée to a 2–3mm thickness. Using a 3.5 or 4cm fluted pastry cutter, stamp out as many discs as possible from the sheet of pastry. Make the sablés as follows:

Raspberry jam Place the desired number of pastry discs on a baking sheet and moisten lightly with a pastry brush dipped in cold water. Cut a hole in the centre of half of the discs with a 1.5cm pastry cutter, and place them on top of the solid discs. Use a coffee spoon to fill the cavities with raspberry jam, then brush the pastry borders with eggwash. Note that as these are double thickness sablés, they will need longer in the oven.

Almond Place the required number of pastry discs on a baking sheet, brush with eggwash and arrange 5 or 6 almonds on each one.

Chantilly cream with berries Place the desired number of pastry discs on a baking sheet and brush with eggwash. Create a pattern by pressing and sliding the back of a fork over the surface (see photo).

illustrated on previous page

Coffee Place the required number of pastry discs on a baking sheet. Dissolve the coffee in 1 tbsp barely tepid water. Brush each disc generously with coffee, then make a pattern by pressing and sliding the back of a fork over the surface (see photo).

Apricot jam Roll the remaining 100g pâte sablée into a sausage, about 3 cm diameter. Cut into 6 equal pieces and roll each one into a ball between your palms. Flatten slightly, then push your index finger into the centre to make a small hollow. Fill with apricot jam just before baking.

To bake the sablés Preheat the oven to 170°C/Gas 3. Bake the sablés for 6 – 10 minutes, depending on their thickness. If you prefer them with more colour, increase the oven setting to 180°C/Gas 4 for the last minute or two. Transfer to a wire rack to cool.

To finish the sablés When cold, pipe chantilly cream on the appropriate sablés and arrange blueberries or clusters of redcurrants on top. Sprinkle the almond sablés with icing sugar. Arrange all the sablés on a large plate and serve.

The bases can be made a day ahead – just pipe on the cream and decorate with fruit at the last moment. To vary the shapes, use oval, rectangular or other shaped pastry cutters. Allow 15g pastry for each sablé.

serves 8

This elegant, light dessert was created by my son Alain at The Waterside Inn. You can prepare the different elements a day ahead, ready to assemble at the last moment.

460g pâte sablée (see page 76)
60g caster sugar
400g fresh or frozen blueberry purée
  (bought is fine)
juice of ½ lemon
8g leaf gelatine

30ml crème de myrtilles liqueur (optional)
120g Italian meringue (see page 294)
150g double cream, softly whipped
30g caster sugar, to glaze
40 fresh blueberries
8 mint sprigs

First make the blueberry coulis. Put 50ml water and the sugar in a small pan, dissolve over a low heat, then bring to the boil to make a syrup. Set aside until cold. Mix the cold syrup with 100g of the blueberry purée, add the lemon juice and refrigerate until ready to use.

For the mousse, soak the gelatine in cold water to cover. Heat 50g of the blueberry purée in a pan. As it begins to bubble, take the pan off the heat, squeeze the gelatine to remove excess water, then stir it into the hot purée until dissolved. Stir in the remaining 250g blueberry purée with a whisk. Add the liqueur if using, then delicately fold in the meringue with the whisk. Finally fold in the whipped cream using a flexible spatula.

Place 8 pastry rings, 8cm diameter and 4cm deep, on a baking sheet lined with cling film. Fill them with blueberry mousse and refrigerate for 3 hours (or freeze for 1 hour) until set.

For the sablés, preheat the oven to 170°C/Gas 3. Roll out the pastry to a 2–3mm thickness and cut out 16 discs with a 9cm fluted pastry cutter. Using a 3cm plain cutter, cut a hole in the centre of half of the discs. Transfer the sablés to a baking sheet with a palette knife and bake for 6–8 minutes until pale blonde. Sprinkle the discs that have a hole with a pinch of caster sugar and heat with a cook's blowtorch until melted and very lightly caramelised.

To serve, spoon the chilled blueberry coulis onto 8 plates. To unmould each mousse, lightly run a blowtorch around the outside of the ring and release onto a plain sablé. Top with a glazed sablé and arrange a few blueberries and a mint sprig in the centre. Slide a palette knife under the sablés and place in the centre of the coulis. Serve immediately.

I adore the airy quality of puff pastry and find freshly baked palmiers or couques impossible to resist. It is the king of pastries — just as turbot is the king of fish. Do try making your own puff pastry — it really isn't difficult. If you have time (about 80 minutes plus resting), opt for classic puff; otherwise you can make rough puff, which takes just 20 minutes plus resting. Classic puff pastry is the thoroughbred and gives perfect results. Rough puff tastes as good, but rises slightly less during cooking. The choice is yours — the most important thing is to have a go! Puff pastry can be frozen successfully for several weeks — in usable portions so you can take out as much as you need. It is suited to both savoury and sweet confections. Glaze it with eggwash before baking and you will be rewarded with a brilliant shine. Puff pastry rises in the oven in a most impressive fashion, but unlike a soufflé, it will retain its imposing stature and lightness as it cools.

puff pastry

classic puff pastry

makes 1.2 kg

Wrapped in cling film, then in greaseproof
paper, puff pastry will keep for at least a week
in the fridge, and for several weeks in the
freezer, though it is best to adjust the method
slightly if you are freezing it (see overleaf).

500g plain flour
12g salt
25ml white wine vinegar
200ml ice-cold water
50g melted butter
400g very cold butter

Put the flour in a mound on a cool work surface (ideally marble) and make a well in the middle. Put the salt, wine vinegar, water and melted butter into the well.

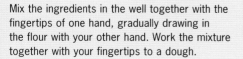

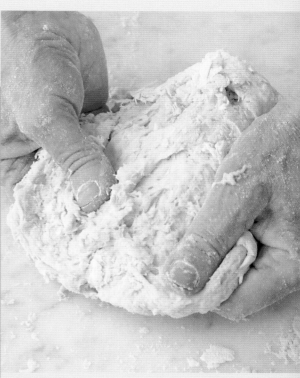

When the pastry is almost amalgamated, push it with the palm of your hand 5 or 6 times until it is completely homogeneous. Roll the pastry into a ball, wrap in cling film and refrigerate for 2 hours.

Mix the ingredients in the well together with the fingertips of one hand, gradually drawing in the flour with your other hand. Work the mixture together with your fingertips to a dough.

continued overleaf

Lightly flour the clean surface. Roll out the ball of pastry, rolling the 4 corners further out to make 4 large flaps.

Lightly flour the work surface again. Roll the pastry away from you to make a rectangle about 70 x 40cm. Fold the ends over the middle to make 3 layers. This is the first turn.

Bash the cold butter several times with the rolling pin to make it pliable and place in the centre of the pastry. Fold the flaps over the butter to enclose it.

Give the pastry a quarter-turn and once more roll it away from you into a 70 x 40 cm rectangle, then fold it into 3 layers again. This is the second turn. Wrap the pastry in cling film and refrigerate for 1 hour to relax and firm up.

Repeat the rolling out and folding twice more to make two more turns and refrigerate the pastry again for an hour. Make another 2 turns (a total of 6 turns) and chill the pastry for an hour. It is now ready to use.

Note At each stage of folding, mark the number of turns with the end of the rolling pin to remind you which stage you are at.

If you intend to freeze the pastry, it is best to do only 4 turns before freezing, and make the final 2 turns after thawing, about 1 hour before using the pastry.

rough puff pastry

makes 1.2 kg

This quick puff pastry rises well – almost 75% as much as classic puff pastry, and it saves an incredible amount of time.

500 g plain flour
500 g very cold butter, cut into small cubes
1 tsp salt
250 ml ice-cold water

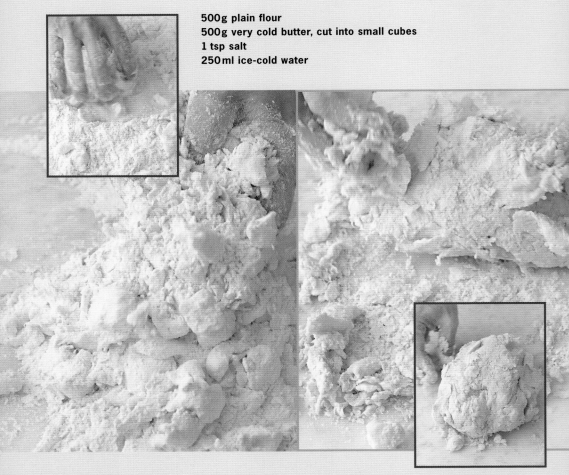

Put the flour in a mound on the work surface and make a well. Put in the butter and salt and work them together with the fingertips of one hand, gradually drawing the flour into the centre with the other hand.

When the cubes of butter have become small pieces and the dough is grainy, gradually add the iced water and mix until it is all incorporated, but don't overwork the dough. Roll it into a ball, wrap in cling film and refrigerate for 20 minutes.

Once you have tried making rough puff pastry, you'll probably opt for this easier method every time. Tightly wrapped in cling film, it will keep for 3 days in the fridge, and for at least 4 weeks in the freezer.

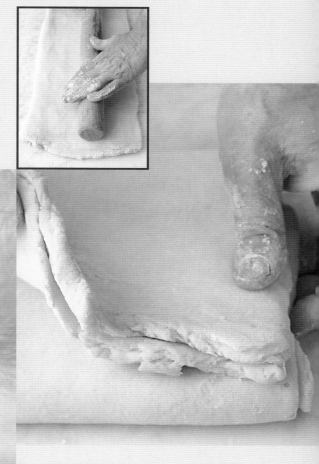

Flour the work surface and roll out the pastry into a 40 x 20cm rectangle. Fold it into three and give it a quarter-turn. Roll the block of pastry into a 40 x 20cm rectangle as before, and fold it into three again. These are the first 2 turns. Wrap the block in cling film and refrigerate it for 30 minutes.

Give the chilled pastry another 2 turns, rolling and folding as before. This makes a total of 4 turns, and the pastry is now ready. Wrap it in cling film and refrigerate for at least 30 minutes before using.

These crisp, light pastry straws are perfect to nibble with pre-dinner drinks. You can prepare the pastry a day ahead, ready to cut and bake at the last moment. They are best served warm from the oven.

olive straws

makes 12

As a variation, replace the olives with anchovies tinned in oil, well drained.

375g puff pastry, either rough puff (see pages 112–3) or classic (see pages 108–11)
15 large green olives, about 3cm long, stuffed with pimentos
eggwash (1 egg yolk mixed with 1 tbsp milk)

On a lightly floured surface, roll the pastry out to a 32 x 15cm rectangle, about 3mm thick. Using a chef's knife, cut the rectangle into 2 pieces, one 14 x 15cm and the other 18 x 15cm. Place on a baking sheet and refrigerate for 10 minutes.

Take the smaller piece of pastry and, starting 1.5cm from the edge, lay 5 olives end to end in a line along the 14cm side of the rectangle. Leave a 2cm space and make another line of 5 olives. Repeat to make 3 lines of olives. Brush all the exposed pastry between the olives with eggwash. Cover with the larger piece of pastry and press the whole surface of the pastry between the olives firmly with your fingertips. Refrigerate for about 20 minutes.

Preheat the oven to 200°C/Gas 6. With a very sharp knife, trim and neaten the edges of the pastry, then cut it crossways into straws about 6mm wide (as illustrated on page 114). Lay the straws flat side down on a baking sheet and bake for 5–6 minutes. As soon as you remove them from the oven, carefully transfer to a wire rack and let cool slightly.

Serve the olive straws, preferably while still warm, on a plate or in a tall goblet.

illustrated (with the cheese straws) on previous page

makes 24

400g puff pastry, either rough puff (see pages 112–3) or classic (see pages 108–11)
eggwash (1 egg yolk mixed with 1 tbsp milk)
80g Emmenthal or Parmesan, freshly grated
1 tsp sweet paprika
pinch of cayenne pepper

On a lightly floured surface, roll out the pastry to a 28 x 12cm rectangle, about 2mm thick. Roll it loosely over the rolling pin and unroll it onto a baking sheet lined with greaseproof paper. Refrigerate for 20 minutes.

Preheat the oven to 180°C / Gas 4. Brush the entire surface of the pastry with eggwash and sprinkle on the grated cheese evenly. Mix the paprika and cayenne together and dust over the surface. Use a chef's knife to trim and neaten the edges of the pastry, then halve it lengthways to make 2 bands, each measuring 14 x 12cm.

Cut each piece into 1cm wide strips, making 24 straws in all. Lift each cheese straw with a palette knife, hold both ends and twist them 6 times in opposite directions to make a spiral. Put the straws on a baking sheet and bake for 5–6 minutes. Remove from the oven and immediately transfer to a wire rack carefully. Leave to cool slightly.

Arrange the cheese straws in a tall goblet or on a plate and serve, preferably while still warm.

Perfect to nibble on with an aperitif, cheese straws are also good served alongside a bowl of chicken consommé.

tomato bavaroise millefeuilles with tomato coulis

serves 6

400g classic puff pastry (see pages 108–11)
2 sheets of leaf gelatine
250 ml tomato pulp (either fresh or from a jar),
  strained if necessary
2 tbsp tomato purée
5 drops of Tabasco
1 tbsp Worcestershire sauce
200 ml double cream, lightly whipped
salt and freshly ground pepper

tomato coulis
150g ripe tomatoes
pinch of powdered pectin

to assemble
3 medium semi-confit tomatoes
  (see page 289)
6 basil sprigs

To make the bavaroise, soak the gelatine in cold water to cover for a few minutes to soften. Meanwhile, heat about a third of the tomato pulp in a saucepan. As soon as it begins to bubble, take off the heat, squeeze the gelatine leaves to remove excess water and add to the hot pulp, stirring with a whisk until dissolved. Put the remaining tomato pulp in a bowl and whisk in the gelatine mixture, then add the tomato purée, Tabasco, Worcestershire sauce and cream. Mix delicately and season generously with salt.

Place 6 oval pastry rings, 8 x 5 cm and 3 cm deep, on a baking sheet lined with greaseproof paper or cling film. Spoon the bavaroise into the rings and level the surface. Chill in the fridge for at least 2 hours. (If you have any bavaroise left over, you'll find it is delicious spread on slices of crusty baguette.)

For the tomato coulis, peel, halve and deseed the fresh tomatoes. Blitz in a blender for 30 seconds, then pass through a chinois into a bowl. Season with salt and pepper to taste, add the pectin and chill.

Roll out the pastry to a rectangle, 2 mm thick. Lift and roll it loosely around the rolling pin, then unroll it onto a lightly greased baking sheet. Refrigerate for 30 minutes.

Preheat the oven to 200°C / Gas 6. Prick the pastry rectangle in about 10 places with a fork. Lay a baking sheet the same size as the rectangle on top of it to encourage the pastry to rise evenly and not too much. Immediately bake in the oven for 10 minutes. Lower the oven setting to 170°C / Gas 3 and bake for another 10 minutes.

Protect your handing with an oven cloth, carefully lift off the top baking sheet and check that the pastry is cooked. If not, return it to the oven for 5 minutes or so. Using a palette knife, slide the pastry sheet onto a wire rack and leave to cool completely.

Transfer the cold pastry to your work surface. Using an oval pastry ring, about 10 x 6.5 cm as a guide, cut out 12 pastry ovals with the tip of a very sharp knife.

Cut 6 ovals, like large petals, from the semi-confit tomatoes. One at a time, lightly run a blowtorch around the bavaroise rings and unmould each one onto a pastry oval. Place a tomato petal on each of the remaining pastry ovals and position on top of the bavaroise. Garnish with a sprig of basil. Spread the tomato coulis onto 6 individual plates. Using a palette knife, lift a millefeuille into the centre of each plate. Press very gently to stabilise the millefeuilles on the coulis and serve at once.

With its summery flavours, this lovely, delicate dish is perfect for lunch or as a dinner party starter. Prepare all the elements a day ahead if you like, but assemble them at the last minute – to keep the pastry crisp.

spinach and pear turnovers with parmesan sauce

serves 4

Delicious with a lightly dressed salad of red chicory and cooked beetroot.

280g puff pastry, either rough puff (see pages
  112–3) or classic (see pages 108–11)
2 very ripe pears
juice of 1 lemon
100g caster sugar
50g butter
250g small spinach leaves, washed and
  stalks removed

salt and freshly ground pepper
30g pine nuts, lightly toasted
eggwash (1 egg yolk mixed with 1 tbsp milk)
2 tbsp dried fennel seeds
150ml béchamel sauce (see page 286)
75ml double cream
75g Parmesan, freshly grated

Peel, quarter and core the pears, then place in a small saucepan. Add the lemon juice, sugar and water to cover and poach gently for 15–20 minutes. Meanwhile, heat the butter in a frying pan, add the spinach and cook for 2–3 minutes, then drain. Tip into a bowl and season. Drain the pears, slice thinly and add to the spinach with the pine nuts. Mix delicately and leave to cool.

Cut the pastry into 4 equal pieces. Roll each one out to a round, 3mm thick, and trim to a neat disc using a 14cm cutter. Divide the pear and spinach mixture among the discs, piling it on the half closest to you and leaving a 1.5cm margin at the edge. Brush this edge with eggwash, then fold the other half of the pastry over the filling to make a turnover and lightly press the edges together. Place on a baking sheet and rest in the fridge for 20 minutes.

When ready to bake, preheat the oven to 200°C/Gas 6. Brush the turnovers with eggwash and lightly score the outer edge. Sprinkle the turnovers with fennel seeds and bake in the oven for 5 minutes. Lower the oven setting to 180°C/Gas 4 and bake for another 15 minutes. Place the cooked turnovers on a wire rack.

Meanwhile, for the sauce, heat the béchamel. As as it starts to bubble, add the cream and simmer gently, stirring with a whisk, for 2–3 minutes. Add half the Parmesan and season.

To serve, place a turnover on each plate. Pour the sauce around and sprinkle with the rest of the Parmesan. Serve at once, as a lunch or light supper with a side salad.

feuilletés of poached egg and mushrooms

serves 6

> Here I love the way the egg yolk runs onto the tarragon as you pierce
> it, releasing the unique aromatic, piquant flavour of this herb.

300g classic puff pastry (see pages 108–11)
eggwash (1 egg yolk mixed with 1 tbsp milk)
80g butter
250g button mushrooms, cleaned and
  thinly sliced
juice of $\frac{1}{2}$ lemon
1 tbsp chopped parsley

salt and freshly ground pepper
3 tbsp white wine vinegar
6 very fresh eggs
36 small tarragon leaves
1 tbsp Dijon mustard
$\frac{1}{2}$ quantity hollandaise sauce (see page 286)

Roll out the pastry on a lightly floured surface to a 4mm thickness and cut out 6 discs
with a 7cm cutter. Lightly moisten a baking sheet with cold water. With a palette knife,
lift the discs onto the baking sheet, spacing them apart. Rest in the fridge for 30 minutes.

Preheat the oven to 180°C/Gas 4. Brush the pastry discs with eggwash. Place a 6cm plain
pastry cutter on the discs and press it lightly into the pastry to mark out lids. With a
knife, lightly score a lattice on the lids and prick them in 4 places with a fork. Bake in the
oven for 15 minutes. As soon as the feuilletés are cooked, cut round the lids with the tip
of a knife and carefully lift them off. Place the feuilletés and lids on a wire rack.

Heat the butter in a medium frying pan and sauté the mushrooms for 5–6 minutes until
tender. Add the lemon juice, chopped parsley and seasoning; keep warm.

For the poached eggs, two-thirds fill a wide saucepan, about 10cm deep, with water and
add the vinegar, but no salt. Bring to the boil. Break an egg into a ramekin, then carefully
tip it into the spot where the water is bubbling. Repeat with another 2 eggs and poach for
about 1½ minutes. Lift out the eggs one at a time with a slotted spoon, press with your
fingertip to check that they are done to your liking, and place in a bowl of lukewarm
water. Poach the other 3 eggs in the same way, then neaten the edges with a sharp knife.

Divide the mushrooms between the pastry cases and lay a poached egg on top. Place each
feuilleté on a warm plate and prop the pastry lid against it. Garnish with the tarragon. Stir
the mustard into the hollandaise, coat each egg with a spoonful and serve immediately.

illustrated on previous page

serves 4

Fresh ginger and tamarind give these scallops a remarkable taste, but the flavourings must be discreet, so don't exceed the quantities specified.

500g classic puff pastry (see pages 108–11)
8 fresh scallops, about 40g each, cleaned
salt and freshly ground pepper
2 tsp tamarind paste
1 tsp very finely grated fresh root ginger
8 spinach leaves, briefly blanched, drained
   and patted dry

750 ml grapeseed oil (or groundnut oil),
   for deep-frying
1 egg
1 tsp groundnut oil
75g very dry breadcrumbs (preferably
   Japanese panko)
1 lemon, cut into quarters
sweet chilli sauce (ready-made), to serve

Put the scallops in a small saucepan, add cold water to just cover and a pinch of salt, and heat until the water reaches 70°C. Immediately turn off the heat and leave the scallops in the poaching water until completely cold. Drain the scallops and dry on kitchen paper.

Cut a deep slit horizontally three-quarters of the way through the middle of each scallop. Mix the tamarind and ginger together, then push a little into each scallop with your finger and coat the outside with the mixture. As each scallop is ready, wrap it in a spinach leaf.

On a lightly floured surface, roll out half the pastry to a band, about 24 cm long, 12 cm wide and 2 mm thick. Lay the scallops on the band, leaving a 2 cm space between each one. Roll out the second piece of pastry to a band of the same dimensions. Brush the exposed pastry round the scallops with a pastry brush dipped in cold water. Lift the other pastry band over the rolling pin and unroll it over the scallop band. Press the pastry all round the scallops firmly with your fingertips to seal. Cut out each pastry-wrapped scallop with a 6 cm plain pastry cutter, place on a lightly floured plate and refrigerate for 20 minutes.

Heat the oil for deep-frying in a suitable pan to 160°C. Break the egg into a shallow dish, add the groundnut oil, season lightly with salt and pepper and beat for 10 seconds with a fork. Coat the pastry-wrapped scallops in the egg mixture, then roll in the breadcrumbs. Drop them all simultaneously into the hot oil and deep-fry for 3–4 minutes until the pastry is golden, cooked and puffed. Lift out with a strainer and drain on kitchen paper.

Serve immediately, with lemon wedges for squeezing and sweet chilli sauce for dipping.

serves 4

Miniature versions of these feuilletés make perfect canapés.

380g classic puff pastry (see pages 108–11)
120g caster sugar
240g salmon fillet, skinned
60ml olive oil
juice of 3 lemons
5g white peppercorns, cracked
salt and freshly ground pepper

240g fresh scallops (about 4 good-sized
    ones), cleaned
15g chives, finely snipped
$1/2$ cucumber
4 dill sprigs
12 caper berries
4 lemon verbena sprigs (optional)

Roll out the pastry on a lightly floured surface to a rectangle, 5mm thick. Using a 10cm pastry cutter, 4cm deep, cut out 4 discs. Spread the sugar evenly on the work surface, lay a pastry disc on the sugar and roll it out until about 12cm in diameter. Place on a baking sheet lined with greaseproof paper. Repeat with the other 3 discs and chill for 30 minutes.

Preheat the oven to 200°C/Gas 6. Lightly moisten a baking sheet with cold water. Place the feuilletés sugared side up on the work surface and trim to 10cm with the cutter. Using a palette knife, lift them onto the baking sheet and bake for 10 minutes. As soon as the tops are nicely caramelised and glazed, lower the oven setting to 180°C/Gas 4 and cook for another 5 minutes. Carefully transfer the feuilletés to a wire rack with a palette knife.

For the salmon tartare, cut the salmon into 3mm dice and place in a bowl with 40ml olive oil, half the lemon juice, half the cracked peppercorns and salt to taste. Toss to mix well. For the scallop tartare, cut the scallops into 3mm dice and place in another bowl with the rest of the olive oil, lemon juice and pepper, and the chives. Season with salt and toss to mix. Leave both the salmon and scallop tartares to marinate for 10 minutes.

Meanwhile, peel and deseed the cucumber and cut into long julienne ribbons. Divide into 4 portions and roll each around the tines of a fork to make a nest.

Put the feuilletés on individual plates. Spoon the scallop tartare into the middle of each one, surround with the salmon tartare and top with a dill sprig. Place a cucumber nest alongside and garnish with caper berries, and verbena if using. Serve at once, as a starter.

herbed monkfish in a puff pastry crust

serves 4

500g classic puff pastry (see pages 108–11)
4 small monkfish tails, about 250g each
1 onion, finely sliced
1 leek, white part only, finely sliced
bouquet garni
salt and freshly ground pepper
80g flat leaf parsley, finely snipped

80g tarragon, finely snipped
12 large spinach leaves, blanched, refreshed
  and drained
4 herb crêpes (see page 290), optional
eggwash (1 egg yolk mixed with 1 tbsp milk)
1 quantity choron sauce (see page 287)

Put the monkfish tails in a wide saucepan, in one layer. Add the onion, leek and bouquet garni. Cover with cold water, season and bring to the boil. Lower the heat so the water is just below simmering and poach the fish for 5 minutes, then turn off the heat. Leave the fish in the poaching liquid to cool completely, then chill for several hours.

Drain the fish and pat dry. Using a filleting knife, make an incision down each tail, without cutting right through, and remove the central bone. Stuff the cavities with some of the herbs; roll the tails in the rest. Wrap each one in 3 spinach leaves, then a crêpe if using.

Roll out a quarter of the pastry on a lightly floured surface to a 2 mm thick rectangle, 6 cm longer than the monkfish tails and wide enough to enclose them. Place a wrapped tail in the centre and cut away the excess pastry to a point at the tail end. Brush the short ends of the pastry with eggwash. Fold one side of the pastry over the tail, pressing firmly, then brush with eggwash and fold the other side over it. Roll out the ends and cut off excess, leaving 4 cm flaps. Brush these with eggwash and fold over the monkfish. Turn the parcels over onto a baking sheet. Prepare the other parcels in the same way. Chill for 20 minutes.

Preheat the oven to 180°C/Gas 4. Brush the pastry with eggwash and score vertical rays lightly with a knife tip along the length. Bake for 20 minutes or until the pastry is cooked.

To serve, using a sharp serrated knife, cut each parcel into 3 medallions, discarding the end pieces of pastry. Arrange on warm plates and spoon a little choron sauce around. Serve at once, with steamed courgettes (ideally round ones), and the rest of the sauce.

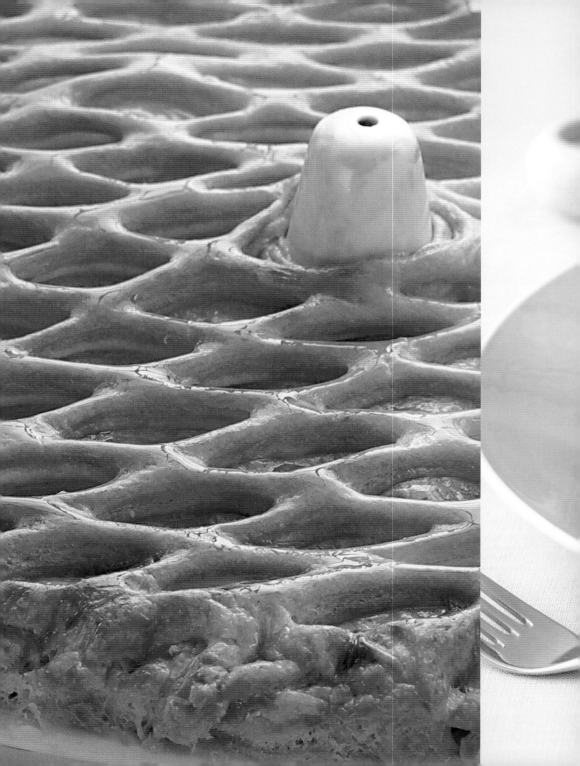

chicken wing and curried mussel pie

serves 8

650g rough puff pastry (see pages 112–3)
24 chicken wings, wing tips removed
bouquet garni
24 baby onions
salt and freshly ground pepper
1 kg fresh mussels, cleaned
200 ml dry white wine
60g shallots, finely chopped

1 thyme sprig
2 bay leaves
75g butter
75g plain flour
200 ml double cream
1 tbsp Madras curry powder
20g flat leaf parsley, finely chopped
eggwash (1 egg yolk mixed with 1 tbsp milk)

For the pie filling, put the chicken wings in a saucepan, add just enough cold water to cover and bring to the boil. Skim the surface, then add the bouquet garni and simmer gently for 45 minutes. Leave to cool in the liquid, then drain, reserving the liquor, and place in a large bowl. Cook the baby onions in a pan of simmering salted water about 5 minutes until just tender, then drain and set aside.

Put the mussels, white wine, shallots, thyme and bay leaves in a saucepan over a high heat and cover with a tight-fitting lid. Cook briskly, shaking the pan and stirring every minute or so until all the mussels have opened. Immediately drain, reserving the liquor, and shell the mussels, discarding any that have not opened. Keep the shelled mussels covered with a damp cloth. Return the liquor to the pan, bring to the boil and let bubble until reduced by half. Strain through a chinois into a bowl and set aside.

Melt the butter in a saucepan, add the flour, stir with a whisk and cook, stirring, over a medium heat for 2 minutes, to make a roux. Off the heat, pour on the reserved chicken and mussel cooking liquors, stirring with a whisk. Now cook, stirring, over a medium heat to make a smooth sauce. As soon as it comes to the boil, stir in the cream and curry powder, and simmer, still stirring, for 10 minutes. Season with salt and pepper to taste.

illustrated on previous page

You can prepare this pie a day ahead, ready to top with pastry and bake before the meal. The unexpected combination of flavours is truly delicious. Serve with freshly cooked okra or green beans tossed in melted butter.

Pour the sauce through a chinois onto the chicken wings. Add the mussels, baby onions and chopped parsley, mixing gently with a spatula. Leave until cold, then transfer to a pie dish with a funnel placed in the centre. Cover with cling film and refrigerate until you are ready to bake the pie.

Preheat the oven to 180°C/Gas 4. Roll out two-thirds of the pastry on a lightly floured surface to the same shape as the pie dish, but slightly larger all round. Brush the edge of the pie dish with eggwash. Loosely roll the pastry round the rolling pin and unroll it over the dish. Using a sharp knife, make a small hole in the centre to expose the funnel. Press the pastry onto the rim of the pie dish with your fingers and brush all over with eggwash.

Roll the remaining pastry into a 30 x 14 cm band. Run a lattice pastry cutter along the length of the band, then gently pull it open widthways into a 26 cm wide lattice. Roll it loosely round the rolling pin and unroll it over the pie; cut off the excess pastry around the dish with scissors. (If you do not have a lattice cutter, you can decorate the top with leaves cut from the pastry trimmings.) Place the pie in the fridge to rest for 20 minutes.

Very delicately brush the lattice with eggwash, then bake in the oven for 1 hour. Serve soon after you take the pie from the oven, with okra or green beans.

Vary the mushrooms according to the season and availability.

460g classic puff pastry (see pages 108–11)
eggwash (1 egg yolk mixed with 1 tbsp milk)
120g butter
150g girolles (golden chanterelles), trimmed
   and wiped clean
100g trompettes de la mort (black trumpets),
   trimmed

30g shallot, very finely chopped
salt and freshly ground pepper
1 sole, about 600g, filleted and skinned
30g flat leaf parsley, snipped
juice of 1 lemon

To prepare the bouchées, roll out the pastry on a lightly floured surface to a rectangle, 3mm thick. Using a 9cm pastry cutter, cut out 8 discs and transfer with a palette knife to a baking sheet lined with greaseproof paper. Chill for 30 minutes.

Preheat the oven to 180°C / Gas 4. Arrange 4 pastry discs on a baking sheet and brush with eggwash. Using a 7cm pastry cutter, cut out the centres of the other 4 discs and discard them. With a palette knife, invert the pastry rings onto the whole discs, press lightly with your fingertips to adhere, then brush the rings with eggwash. Prick the centre of the bouchées once with a fork and bake for 20 minutes. Cut round the inside of the rims with a knife tip and remove the excess pastry. Transfer the bouchées to a wire rack.

For the filling, heat 40g butter in a small frying pan and cook the girolles over a medium heat for 3 minutes. Add the trompettes de la mort and cook for a further 5 minutes. Add the shallot, season to taste and keep warm.

Cut the sole fillets into 1cm wide strips. Heat the remaining butter in a frying pan until foaming, then add the sole strips (goujonettes) and cook for 3 minutes, turning them over every minute. Add the mushrooms, parsley and lemon juice, season and mix delicately.

Generously fill the bouchées with the sole and mushroom mixture. Put them on warm plates and serve at once, with steamed pak choi or a salad of mixed leaves.

sea bass en croûte with mousseline sauce

serves 6

1 sea bass, about 1.6 kg
100g fresh tender fennel fronds (ideally),
   or a few thyme sprigs
900g classic puff pastry (see pages 108–11)
4 herb crêpes (see page 290), optional

8 large spinach leaves, blanched for 20 seconds
   and wrapped in a damp tea towel
eggwash (1 egg yolk mixed with 1 tbsp milk)
a little clarified butter (see page 297), to glaze
1 quantity mousseline sauce (see page 287)

If you haven't persuaded the fishmonger to do so for you, prepare the sea bass. Scrape off the scales with the back of a knife and cut off the side and dorsal fins with scissors. Lay the fish on one side and, using a filleting knife, open it up through its back to the belly, gliding the knife over the bones. Repeat on the underside of the bones. Use the tip of the scissors to cut through the backbone close to the head and the tail. Pull out the whole backbone; the guts will come away with it. Place the tip of the scissors inside the fish and remove the gills, then trim the end of the tail.

Rinse the sea bass under a trickle of cold running water. Sponge it inside and out with kitchen paper, then season lightly with salt and put the fennel fronds or thyme into the cavity. Cover the fish with cling film and refrigerate.

Preheat the oven to 200°C/Gas 6. Lightly flour the work surface and roll out 40% of the pastry into a rectangle about 50 x 15 cm. Roll the pastry loosely round the rolling pin and unroll it onto a chilled 60 x 40 cm baking sheet.

If using crêpes, lay two along the centre of the pastry, overlapping them slightly so they cover almost the whole length. Cover with 4 blanched spinach leaves, lay the sea bass on top and bring the sides of the spinach up over the fish. Cover with the rest of the leaves to wrap the fish completely in spinach. Now bring the crêpes up over the fish and fill any gaps with pieces cut from the remaining crêpes. Don't overlap them more than a mere fraction; the fish should be enclosed in a single layer of crêpe. Brush the puff pastry around the fish with eggwash.

illustrated on pages 136 – 7

This regal dish take times, but all the elements can be prepared ahead.
Then all you need to do is take the fish in its pastry crust from the fridge
to the oven about 40 minutes before you want to serve it.

Roll out the remaining pastry into a 55 x 20 cm rectangle, roll it loosely round the rolling
pin and, starting at the head, unroll it over the fish towards the tail to cover it completely.
Leave to rest in the fridge for 20 minutes.

With a very sharp, small pointed knife, cut off the excess pastry around the fish, leaving
a 2 – 3 cm wide border. Press lightly all round the border with your fingertips to seal it.
Brush the whole surface of the pastry with eggwash. With the knife tip, make very light
incisions on the pastry to look like fish scales. Draw eyes on the head and mark rays on
the head, tail and all round the border. Bake for 10 minutes, then lower the oven setting
to 180°C / Gas 4 and cook for another 25 minutes.

Use a wide palette knife to slide the parcel carefully onto a wire rack. Leave to stand for
5 – 10 minutes before serving. Brush the pastry with a little clarified butter to give it an
extra shine.

Present the fish whole on a platter to impress your guests, then cut into slices using a
very sharp serrated knife. Lift onto individual plates and pour on some mousseline sauce.
Serve the rest in a sauceboat.

The crêpes ensure a crisper crust, as they prevent the steam from
the fish making the pastry soggy, but you can omit these provided
you still wrap the sea bass in spinach leaves.

These individual chicken pies are perfect for a special family lunch or supper with friends. Make the filling ahead, ready to assemble, glaze and bake the pies just before serving.

individual chicken pies

serves 4

400g classic puff pastry (see pages 108–11)
1 free-range chicken, about 1.4kg, boned and cut into 8 pieces, carcass reserved
50g clarified butter (see page 297)
2 medium onions, quartered
150g tomatoes, peeled, deseeded and diced
bouquet garni
salt and freshly ground pepper
150ml dry white wine
50g plain flour

140g pork belly, derinded and cut into large lardons
600ml chicken stock (freshly made or good ready-made)
150g carrots, cut into thick rounds
150g broccoli florets
30g butter
100g field or Portobello mushrooms, quartered
eggwash (1 egg yolk mixed with 1 tbsp milk)

Preheat the oven to 180°C/Gas 4. Break the chicken carcass into pieces. Heat the clarified butter in a large deep frying pan. Add the chicken pieces and chopped carcass and colour them lightly over a medium heat. Add the onions, tomatoes and bouquet garni, season lightly with salt and cook for a few minutes. Pour in the wine, cover the pan with a lid and simmer gently for 15 minutes.

Meanwhile, scatter the flour on a baking tray and toast in the oven for 5 minutes. Blanch the lardons in boiling salted water for 5 minutes, then drain and refresh in cold water; drain and pat dry.

Remove only the chicken pieces from the pan, place in a bowl and cover with a damp tea towel. Sprinkle the toasted flour into the frying pan, stirring as you go, then add the chicken stock. Bring to the boil, stirring occasionally, and cook for 20 minutes, skimming the surface from time to time.

In the meantime, cook the carrots in boiling salted water for 6 minutes, then drain and refresh in cold water; drain. Blanch the broccoli for 30 seconds, then drain and refresh.

Heat the butter in a frying pan, add the lardons and fry until golden, then tip into a bowl. Add the mushrooms to the same pan, sauté for 2–3 minutes and add to the lardons.

illustrated on previous page

Strain the sauce over the chicken pieces. Add the carrots, lardons, mushrooms and broccoli, mix delicately with a wooden spoon and season with salt and pepper. Divide the chicken, sauce and vegetables between 4 individual pie dishes, 14 cm in diameter and 4 cm deep. Leave at room temperature until cold, then refrigerate for at least an hour.

To assemble, on a lightly floured surface roll out one-quarter of the pastry to a 15–16 cm disc, 3 mm thick. Brush the top edge of one pie dish with eggwash and cover with the pastry disc. Repeat with the other 3 pies and place in the fridge for 20 minutes.

Cut off the excess pastry overhanging the dishes with scissors and brush the top of the pies with eggwash. Roll out the pastry trimmings to a 1.5 mm thickness and cut out thin crescents with a 4.5 cm fluted pastry cutter. Arrange 7 crescents round the edge of each pie and brush them with eggwash. Use a sharp knife to cut a small hole in the centre of the pies, then bake at 180°C/Gas 4 for 30 minutes. Put the pies on individual plates and serve piping hot, with a salad or green vegetable.

serves 4

I like to serve these rustic little pies with red cabbage braised with some chopped apple, and scattered with walnuts and grapes to serve.

640g classic puff pastry (see pages 108–11)
500g pork chine, boned
80g shallots, finely chopped
200ml white wine (preferably Riesling)
2 tbsp groundnut oil

30g parsley, snipped
30g dried breadcrumbs
2 hard-boiled eggs, chopped
salt and freshly ground pepper
eggwash (1 egg yolk mixed with 1 tbsp milk)

To make the filling, cut the pork into strips, 1cm wide and 4cm long. Combine the pork, shallots, white wine and oil in a bowl. Mix well, cover with cling film and refrigerate for several hours.

To assemble, mix the parsley, breadcrumbs and eggs into the pork filling and season with salt and pepper. On a lightly floured surface, roll out 120g of the pastry to an 18 x 12 cm rectangle. Spoon one-quarter of the filling into the middle of the pastry, in a 10 cm long band. Brush the edges of the pastry with eggwash. Fold one side of the pastry over the filling and brush this with eggwash, then fold over the other side of the pastry. Roll out the 2 ends of the pastry and cut off the excess, leaving a 3 cm flap at each end. Brush these with eggwash and fold over the filling, pulling them lightly. Invert the parcel onto a baking sheet.

Roll out 40g of the pastry to a rectangle the same size as the parcel. Neaten the edges with a chef's knife. Brush the top of the parcel with eggwash and lift the pastry rectangle onto it, using a palette knife. Make another 3 parcels in the same way and chill for 30 minutes.

Preheat the oven to 180°C/Gas 4. Brush the tops of the parcels with eggwash. Using a knife tip, mark rays at an angle from the middle, then cut a small hole in the centre with a sharp knife. Bake the parcels for 20 minutes. Lower the oven setting to 170°C/Gas 3 and cook for another 10 minutes. Lift the puffs onto a wire rack with a palette knife.

Serve the puffs hot, with braised red cabbage or a leafy salad if you prefer.

beef and ale pies

serves 4

720g rough puff pastry (see pages 112–3)
200g onions, cut into 2cm cubes
200g medium carrots, cut into 2cm chunks
750g braising beef, cut into 3cm cubes
60g plain flour, seasoned with 10g salt
100ml groundnut oil

400ml brown ale (such as Newcastle brown)
400ml rich beef stock (good ready-made is fine)
bouquet garni
250g button mushrooms, quartered
salt and freshly ground pepper
eggwash (1 egg yolk mixed with 1 tbsp milk)

For the pie filling, put the onions in a small saucepan, add just a little water and cook for 5 minutes. Cook the carrots in the same way, for 10 minutes. Leave the vegetables in their cooking water. Roll the beef cubes in the seasoned flour. Heat the oil in a frying pan over a high heat and fry the beef for 3–4 minutes until lightly coloured.

Using a slotted spoon, transfer the meat to a large heavy-based saucepan. Drain the onions and carrots, then add to the meat with the ale. Bring to a simmer over a medium heat, skim, then add the beef stock. Bring back to a simmer, skim again, then add the bouquet garni. Simmer gently, uncovered, for 1¾ hours. Add the mushrooms and cook for another 15 minutes. By now, the cooking juices should have reduced by at least half and become rich in flavour and colour. Discard the bouquet garni and adjust the seasoning. Divide the filling between 4 oval pie dishes, about 17 x 14cm and 4cm deep. Leave until cold, then chill for at least an hour (or overnight if preparing ahead).

Preheat the oven to 180°C/Gas 4. On a lightly floured surface, roll out 130g pastry to the same shape but slightly larger than the top of the pie dishes. Brush the edge of a dish with eggwash. Loosely roll the pastry round the rolling pin and unroll it onto the pie dish. Press the pastry edge onto the rim of the dish with your fingertips and cut off the excess with a knife. Cut a small hole in the centre with a sharp knife and brush the pastry with eggwash.

Roll 50g pastry into a long band, 2cm wide. Lay on the rim of the pie, brush with eggwash and score with a knife tip. Score a pattern on top of the pie if you like. Prepare the other 3 pies in the same way and chill for 20 minutes. Bake the pies for 35 minutes, then serve.

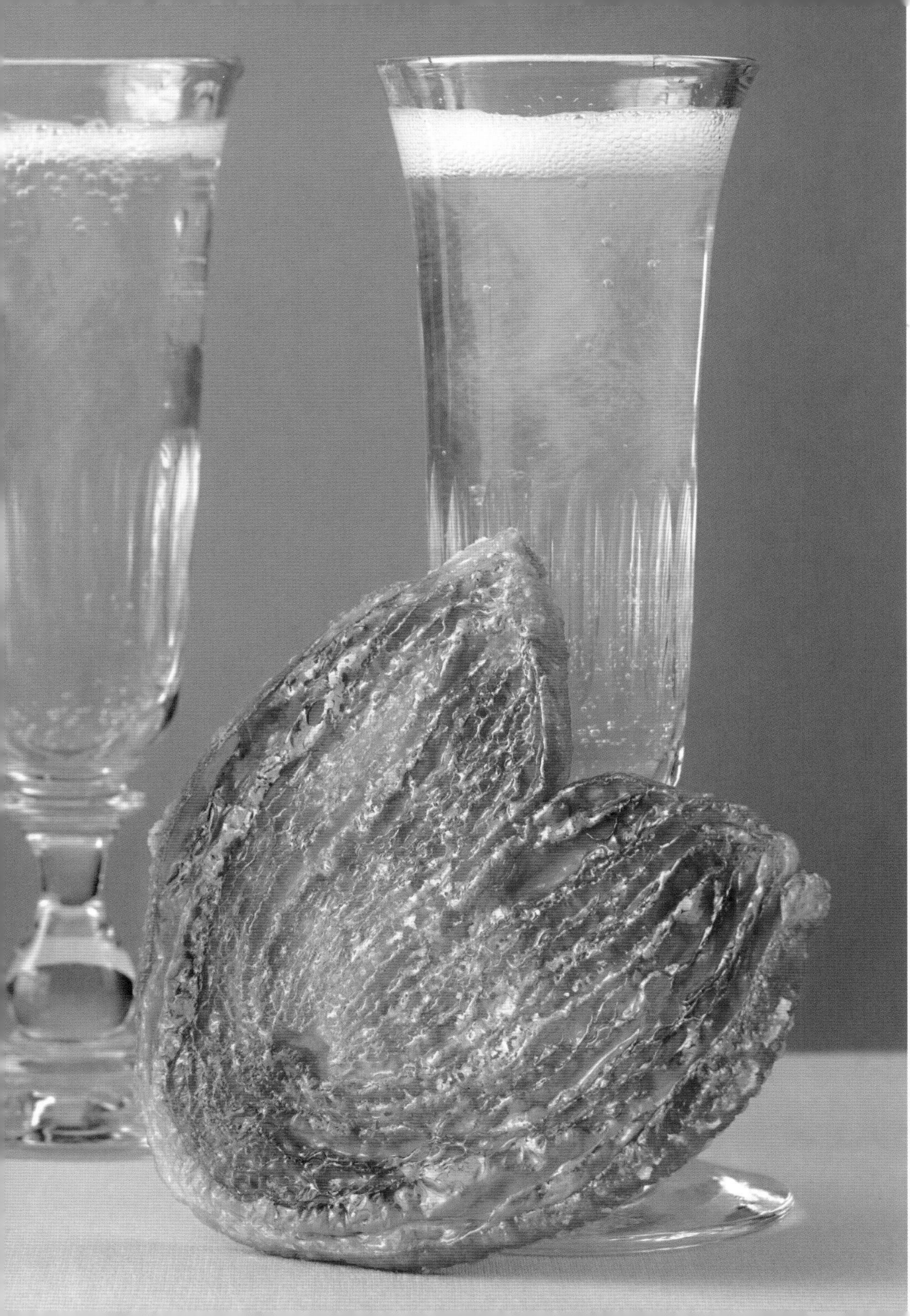

couques

makes 20

These crisp little pastries are perfect petits fours, or you can serve them with ice cream. I sometimes pipe a little crème pâtissière into the centres through the side, using a small plain nozzle – a real treat.

300g classic puff pastry (see pages 108–11)
200g caster sugar

Roll out the pastry to a 5 mm thickness. Using a 3 cm pastry cutter, cut out about 20 discs and arrange them on a baking sheet lined with greaseproof paper. Spread a 5 mm thick layer of caster sugar on the work surface. Put one pastry disc on the sugar and roll it lightly, applying very little pressure, into an oval. Turn the pastry over onto the sugar and roll it lightly again into an oval 5 cm long, 3 cm wide and 3 mm thick. Dip a pastry brush in cold water and lightly moisten a baking sheet. Put the pastry oval on the baking sheet, sugared side up. Repeat with the rest of the pastry to make about 20 discs, reforming the layer of sugar from time to time. Refrigerate the pastry ovals for 30 minutes.

Preheat the oven to 180°C/Gas 4. Bake the couques for 5 minutes until the sugar has caramelised to make an attractive glaze on top. Immediately lower the oven setting to 170°C/Gas 3 and bake for another 2–3 minutes. The couques nearest the corners of the baking sheet will cook and caramelise faster than the rest, so remove them with a palette knife and transfer to a wire rack, leaving the others to cook a little longer. As soon as they are done, lift them onto the wire rack, or the sugar will stick them like glue to the baking sheet as it cools.

Arrange the couques on a platter and serve as petits fours with tea or coffee, or with ice cream.

illustrated (with the palmiers) on previous page

250g classic puff pastry, given only 4 turns
  (see pages 108–11)
about 150g icing sugar, sifted
about 75g granulated sugar

Dust the work surface generously with icing sugar and give the pastry its final 2 turns on this surface, to reach a total of 6 turns. Wrap it in cling film and refrigerate for 30 minutes.

Dust the work surface with a veil of icing sugar mixed with some granulated sugar and roll the pastry out to a 35 cm square, 3 mm thick. Trim the edges neatly with a chef's knife and cut the square through the middle to make 2 rectangles or bands, each 35 x 17.5 cm.

Take one of the bands and fold the long ends towards the middle without letting them touch. Repeat this folding (again bringing the ends to the middle), then finally fold the 2 long ends over themselves without letting them touch, to make a total of 4 thicknesses. Fold the other pastry band in the same way. Refrigerate for at least 30 minutes.

Preheat the oven to 180°C / Gas 4. Using a small, very sharp knife, cut the folded pastry bands into 5 mm slices and lay in staggered rows on a lightly greased baking sheet, spacing them about 6 cm apart. Bake for 8–10 minutes until golden brown, turning them over after 6 minutes. This is particularly important for the palmiers nearest the corners of the baking sheet, as they will cook more quickly.

As soon as the palmiers are cooked, transfer to a wire rack using a palette knife, but don't lay them on top of each other or they will stick together as they cool. Eat the same day.

Serve as petits fours, or make larger palmiers to serve with apple compote.

apple and passion fruit tartlets

serves 6

I adore these tartlets – the passion fruit enhances the flavour
of the apple in a most unexpected way.

380g classic puff pastry (see pages 108–11)
180g crème pâtissière (see page 292)
3 medium apples (preferably Cox's)
60g caster sugar
3 passion fruit

On a lightly floured surface, roll out the pastry to a 2mm thickness. Using a 12cm pastry cutter, cut out 6 discs. Brush a baking sheet with a little cold water and lift the pastry discs onto it with a palette knife. Refrigerate for 20 minutes.

Preheat the oven to 180°C/Gas 4. Prick the pastry discs in 5 places with a fork. Divide the crème pâtissière between them and spread it evenly, leaving a narrow margin around the edge.

Peel the apples with a swivel peeler. Cut in half and remove the cores, then thinly slice each half. Arrange a sliced apple half over the crème pâtissière on each disc, radiating from the centre.

Bake for 15 minutes, then sprinkle generously with the caster sugar and cook for another 5 minutes. Take the tartlets out of the oven and immediately lift them onto a wire rack with a palette knife.

To serve, halve the passion fruit and scrape out the pulp and seeds, using a teaspoon, directly onto the tartlets. Serve on individual plates.

To enjoy these tartlets at their best, serve them warm,
about 10 minutes after they come out of the oven.

tart tatin

serves 4–6

200g classic puff pastry (see pages 108–11)
5 medium apples, not too ripe (preferably
   Braeburn or Cox's)
juice of $\frac{1}{2}$ lemon
120g butter, slightly softened
160g caster sugar

Peel the apples, cut them in half and remove the cores. Sprinkle the fruit with lemon juice. Spread the butter evenly over the base of a tatin mould or a heavy ovenproof 22–24 cm diameter frying pan, 6 cm deep, to form a thick layer. Sprinkle on the sugar and arrange the apples rounded side-down in the pan.

Roll out the pastry on a lightly floured surface to a round, about 3 mm thick and 2 cm wider than the diameter of the mould or frying pan. Prick the pastry in 8–10 places with a fork. Roll it loosely onto the rolling pin, then unroll it over the apples. Cut off any excess pastry with scissors, leaving a 1 cm border all round the edge. Refrigerate for at least 20 minutes.

Preheat the oven to 180°C/Gas 4. Place the frying pan over a medium heat for 10–15 minutes until the butter and sugar have amalgamated and bubbled to a lovely pale amber caramel. Use a small palette knife to lift the edge of the pastry all round to check that the butter and sugar have caramelised evenly. Place in the oven for about 25 minutes until the pastry is cooked.

Take the tart from the oven and quickly invert it onto a serving plate, taking care not to burn yourself. The pastry will now be underneath and the fruit on top. The apples may have moved slightly – use the tip of a small knife to reposition them if necessary. Serve at once, taking care as the caramel topping will be very hot. Delicious with cinnamon ice cream or crème fraîche.

illustrated on previous page

serves 4

As a change, try flavouring the filling for these turnovers with
vanilla or orange blossom water instead of cinnamon.

360g classic puff pastry (see pages 108–11)
2 apples (preferably Cox's), about 400g in total
juice of 1 lemon
60g caster sugar
$^1/_2$ tsp ground cinnamon
eggwash (1 egg yolk mixed with 1 tbsp milk)
20g icing sugar, to glaze

For the filling, peel, quarter and core the apples, then cut the flesh into tiny pieces. Place
in a saucepan with the lemon juice, caster sugar, cinnamon and 50ml water. Bring to a
low simmer, cover and cook gently for 15 minutes. Stir the apples with a whisk. Increase
the heat and, still stirring with the whisk, cook for 2 minutes to dry out the compote and
give it a semi-firm consistency. Take off the heat and leave to cool completely.

For the turnovers, on a lightly floured surface roll out the pastry to a 45 x 16cm rectangle,
3mm thick. Turn it so a long side is parallel to you and spoon the cold apple compote into
4 mounds along this side, starting 4cm in from the edge and leaving a 6cm space between
each mound. Dip a pastry brush in cold water and brush the pastry around the mounds,
then fold the half of the pastry furthest from you over the compote, making sure the edges
are well aligned. Lightly press the pastry all round the mounds with your fingertips.

Position a fluted 10cm diameter pastry cutter so that half is on the pastry and half on the
work surface, and cut out 4 semi-circles enclosing the compote mounds. Place these on
a baking sheet lightly moistened with cold water. Refrigerate for 20 minutes.

Preheat the oven to 200°C/Gas 6. Brush the tops of the turnovers with eggwash and
score the pastry very lightly with a knife tip. Bake the turnovers for 18 minutes. Increase
the oven setting to 220°C/Gas 7, dust the turnovers with a veil of icing sugar and bake
for another 2–3 minutes to glaze. As soon as the tops are caramelised, transfer to a wire
rack with a palette knife. Serve the apple turnovers warm, but not searingly hot.

feuilletés with warm cherries and mint ice cream

serves 4

A simple but fabulous dessert – cherries and freshly made
mint ice cream are perfect partners.

260g rough puff pastry (see pages 112–3)
100g caster sugar

mint ice cream
500ml crème anglaise, infused with
40g chopped mint leaves instead of
vanilla (see page 292)

poached cherries
48 cherries, stoned
60g butter
60g caster sugar

to serve
4 clusters of cherries

To make the feuilletés, on a lightly floured surface, roll the pastry out to a rectangle, 5mm
thick. Using a 10cm pastry cutter, cut out 4 discs. Lightly spread the sugar on the surface.
Lay a pastry disc on the sugar and roll it out until 12cm in diameter. Lift onto a baking
sheet lined with greaseproof paper. Repeat with the other 3 discs and chill for 30 minutes.

Preheat the oven to 200°C/Gas 6. Turn the pastry discs sugared side up and trim to 10cm
with the cutter. Lift them onto a baking sheet lightly moistened with cold water using a
palette knife. Lightly press a plain 7cm pastry cutter onto the middle of each disc to mark
a rim (the centres will form the lids). Bake for 10 minutes or until the tops are glazed
and nicely caramelised. Lower the oven setting to 180°C/Gas 4 and cook for another
5 minutes. As soon as you take the feuilletés out of the oven, run a knife tip around the rim
and lift off the lids. Use a palette knife to transfer the feuilletés and lids to a wire rack.

For the mint ice cream, leave the crème anglaise until cold, then pass it through a chinois
and churn in an ice-cream maker to the desired consistency.

For the cherries, melt the butter in a deep frying pan and tip in the sugar. Add the cherries
and toss lightly over a medium heat for 3 minutes until hot and barely half-cooked, then
drain, reserving the juices. Return the juices to the pan and reduce until syrupy.

Place a warm feuilleté on each plate. Divide the cherries between them and moisten with
a little of the reduced syrup. Place a quenelle (or scoop) of mint ice cream on top of each
one and a cluster of cherries alongside. Serve right away.

serves 8

You can make this ahead and freeze it before glazing and baking.
To serve, allow to thaw for 30 minutes, then brush with eggwash,
score and bake, allowing an extra 10 minutes.

500g classic puff pastry (see pages 108–11)
250g almond cream (see page 295)
50g crème pâtissière (see page 292)
1 tbsp rum (optional)
eggwash (1 egg yolk mixed with 1 tbsp milk)
30g icing sugar, to glaze

Cut the pastry into 2 pieces, one weighing 300g and the other 200g. On a lightly floured surface, roll out the smaller piece to a round, giving it several quarter-turns, until you have a 24 cm diameter disc, 3 mm thick. Roll it loosely onto the rolling pin, then unroll it onto a baking sheet lightly brushed with cold water to form the pithiviers base. Roll out the larger piece of pastry for the top in the same way to make a 24 cm disc, 4 mm thick.

To assemble the pithiviers, mix the almond cream and crème pâtissière together and flavour with the rum if you wish. Spoon the mixture into the middle of the pastry base and spread it evenly with the spoon, leaving a 3–4 cm margin around the edge. Brush the exposed pastry with eggwash. Lift the other pastry disc over the top and press the edges together firmly with your fingertips to seal. Refrigerate for 30 minutes.

Press a pithiviers marker or 16 cm flan ring onto the pithiviers. Use a knife to cut the pastry extending outside the marker into small, regular 'petals'. Remove the excess pastry and lift off the marker or flan ring. Brush the whole surface of the pastry with eggwash. Using a knife tip, score curved rays, 1 mm deep, arcing from the centre of the pastry out to the edge. Mark the outside petals with diagonal lines.

Preheat the oven to 200°C / Gas 6. Bake the pithiviers for 10 minutes, then reduce the oven setting to 160°C / Gas 2 1/2 and bake for another 25 minutes. Turn the oven setting back up to 200°C / Gas 6. Immediately dust the pithiviers with icing sugar and return it to the hot oven for 2–3 minutes to give an attractive glaze. Serve the pithiviers warm, on its own or with crème anglaise (see page 292) if you prefer.

I love concocting pâtés en croûte, and as the son and grandson of charcutiers, I cannot betray my origins! I prefer to use lard for the pastry, as I find butter too delicate and self-effacing. The dough must be prepared a day ahead, or at least several hours in advance. Take it out of the fridge an hour before using, so that it becomes more malleable and easier to line the mould. Be generous with the spices when seasoning your forcemeat, as they will be less prevalent once cooked and cooled. If you want to add a personal touch to these recipes, try adding some pitted green olives, cooked wild mushrooms or toasted pine nuts; fresh juniper berries are a great addition to game terrines. Provided it hasn't been cut, a pâté en croûte will keep for at least a week in the fridge. Serve it cold but not chilled, or the flavours won't sing out. Make sure that accompanying chutneys and condiments are not too vinegary or spicy, or they will detract from the savour of your pâté en croûte.

raised pie pastry

raised pie pastry

makes 950kg

This pastry will keep in the fridge for a week, or in the freezer for 3 months.

500g plain flour
20g salt
200g lard (preferably) or butter, cut into
**   small pieces and slightly softened**
5 egg yolks mixed with 110ml cold water
**   if using lard, 125ml if using butter**

Put the flour on the work surface and make
a well. Place the salt and lard or butter in the
centre. Use your fingertips to mix and soften
the ingredients in the well, gradually drawing
in the flour and mixing with your fingertips.

When the dough has a fine grainy texture, make a well in the middle. Gradually pour the egg yolk and water mixture into the well, mixing with your fingertips.

When the dough is well amalgamated, push it away from you 4 or 5 times with the heel of your hand to make it homogeneous. Roll into a ball, wrap in cling film and refrigerate until needed. If it is in the fridge for a while, take it out an hour before rolling out.

Shape three-quarters of the pastry into a ball and roll it out gently on a lightly floured surface a little, maintaining its round shape. Use your thumbs to form it into a boat shape. Generously flour the inside of the boat and fold it back on itself. Roll the pastry evenly to the size and shape of the oval mould, flouring the inside of the 'boat' from time to time. Once the pastry is the right size and shape, open up the 'boat' and put your fist inside, working the dough gently to the size of the mould.

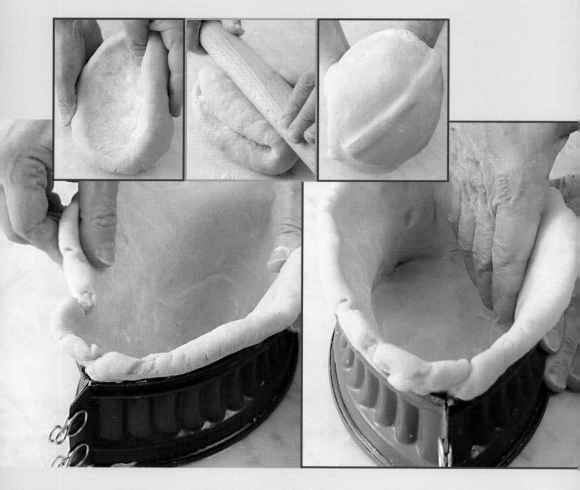

Turn the pastry over and drop it into the buttered mould. Use your fingertips to make it adhere to the sides and base of the mould, and push it right into the corners and base, using a small piece of well-floured pastry to tamp it in. Fill according to the specific recipe.

Roll the remaining pastry into an oval the same size as the top of the mould. Brush the pastry rim above the filling with eggwash, then loosely roll the pastry oval over the rolling pin and unroll it over the top of the pâté. Make sure that the lid adheres perfectly to the border and press firmly to seal. If necessary, cut off any excess pastry with scissors, then crimp the edge by pinching the pastry rim all round between your index finger and thumb to create a decorative border.

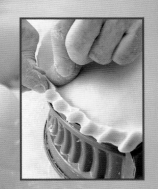

rabbit pâté en croûte

serves 10

For this elegant *pâte à pâté* you will need an oval springform mould, 23 cm long, 14 cm wide and 9 cm high.

900g raised pie pastry (see pages 164–5), not too cold
1 rabbit, preferably wild, about 1.4 kg
200g pork fat, derinded and cut into long strips
300g pork belly, derinded and cut into long strips
100g rabbit livers
75 ml sweet white wine
50 ml Armagnac
150 ml double cream

1 small egg (55g)
1 egg yolk
1 large garlic clove, finely chopped
5g salt
3g freshly ground pepper
7g thyme leaves, finely chopped
150g thinly sliced pork fat, for barding
40g hazelnuts, lightly toasted and skinned
eggwash (1 egg yolk mixed with 1 tbsp milk)

To prepare the rabbit (if your butcher hasn't done so for you), lay it flat on its belly on a board. Using a very sharp boning knife and starting from the head, cut along the line of the spine and cut off the fillets, following the bones. Cut off the shoulders and legs, and debone. Turn the carcass over and remove the small fillets under the backbone. Cut the best of the rabbit fillets into thin strips, wrap in cling film and chill. Chop up the bones and reserve for making the jelly. Cut the rest of the rabbit flesh into small pieces and put into a bowl with the strips of pork fat and belly, and the rabbit livers. Sprinkle with the wine and Armagnac, cover with cling film and leave to marinate in the fridge for 12 hours.

To make the jelly, preheat the oven to 200°C / Gas 6. Drizzle the oil in a roasting pan, add the rabbit bones and roast in the oven for about 20 minutes until browned. Add the onion and carrot and cook for another 5 minutes. Deglaze with the red wine and tip the contents of the pan into a saucepan. Cover with water, add the bouquet garni, celery and leek, bring to the boil and simmer gently for 1 hour, skimming and removing any fat from the surface from time to time. Strain through a chinois into a saucepan and reduce the liquid by almost two-thirds. Season with salt and pepper and set aside to cool.

For the filling, pass the chilled meats through the coarse blade of a mincer. Place in a bowl and stir in the cream, whole egg, yolk, garlic, salt, pepper and thyme, mixing thoroughly.

To assemble the pâté, butter the oval springform pie mould. Roll out three-quarters of the pastry and use to line the mould, following the instructions on page 166. Line the pastry with the thin slices of pork fat, then spoon in a layer of filling, about 2.5 cm thick.

illustrated on pages 168–9

jelly
2 tbsp groundnut oil
1 onion, cut into pieces
1 carrot, cut into pieces
400 ml red wine (ideally Pineau des Charentes)
bouquet garni (with plenty of bay leaves)
2 celery stalks, cut into pieces
1 leek, white part only, cut into pieces
salt and freshly ground pepper

Arrange half the rabbit fillet strips lengthways on the filling, then half the toasted nuts. Make another layer of filling about 2.5 cm thick, lay on the remaining rabbit fillets and nuts, and finish with the rest of the filling. Fold the overhanging pork fat over the filling.

Following the instructions on page 167, roll out the remaining pastry to make the lid, brush the lining pastry rim with eggwash, then apply the lid and press firmly to seal. Cut off any excess pastry, crimp the edge and refrigerate the pâté for at least 2 hours.

To cook the pâté, heat the oven to 180°C/Gas 4. Brush the top of the pastry with egg-wash. Using a knife tip, lightly score rays (or another pattern) on the surface, and, if you like, decorate with 2 or 3 small leaves cut out from the pastry trimmings. Cut a little hole in the middle of the pastry lid and insert a small roll of foil to make a 'chimney'.

Bake for 20 minutes, then lower the oven setting to 160°C/Gas 2½ and bake for another 40 minutes. To check the cooking, insert a trussing needle into the centre of the pâté; if it comes out hot, the pâté is done. Transfer to a wire rack and leave to cool for 2 hours.

To unmould, release the clips and remove the curved sides of the mould. Leave the pâté to cool for another 2 hours (4 hours in all), then remove the chimney and put a cone of greaseproof paper into the aperture. Pour in the almost half-set jelly. Refrigerate the pâté for at least 24 hours before serving.

To serve, cut off and discard the first slice (as it will be mostly pastry). Cut the pâté into neat slices to serve. It will keep well in the fridge for up to a week.

pork and egg pies

makes 2 pies, each serves 4

900g raised pie pastry (see pages 164–5),
   not too cold
800g pork shoulder or chine, boned and
   sinews removed, well chilled
160g salt pork belly, derinded, well chilled
$1/2$ tsp five-spice powder
2 tbsp chopped sage, blanched and refreshed
1 tsp cracked black pepper
8g salt
2 hard-boiled eggs, shelled
4 very thin unsmoked streaky bacon rashers,
   derinded
eggwash (1 egg yolk mixed with 1 tbsp milk)

jelly
2 tbsp groundnut oil
1kg pork bones, chopped
1 uncooked pig's trotter, chopped
2 carrots, cut into pieces
2 onions, each stuck with a clove
large bouquet garni (including a celery stalk)
4 tbsp dry sherry (such as Tio Pepe), optional
salt

For the jelly, preheat the oven to 200°C/Gas 6. Pour the oil into a roasting pan, add the chopped bones, pig's trotter, carrots and onions and roast in the oven for 20 minutes until lightly browned. Transfer the contents of the pan to a saucepan (leaving the oil behind). Pour in enough cold water to cover the bones, then add the bouquet garni and bring to the boil over a medium heat. Skim, lower the heat to keep the liquid at about 80°C and simmer for about 2 hours. Strain the liquid through a chinois into a saucepan and boil to reduce to about 350ml. Take the pan off the heat, add the sherry if you wish, and season with salt to taste. Leave to cool.

For the pie filling, cut the chilled pork meat and belly into small cubes, a bit less than 1cm. Put one-third into a food processor and blitz to a fine purée. In a bowl, mix the purée with the cubed pork and add the spice, sage, pepper and salt. Melt 4 tbsp of the cold jelly, add it to the mixture, mix thoroughly with a wooden spatula, then refrigerate for about 30 minutes.

To assemble, shape 375g of the pastry into a ball and roll it out a little on a lightly floured surface, maintaining the round shape. Use your thumbs to form a well, generously flour the inside and push your fist into the well. Now place the wooden pie mould in the well and turn it upside down. Push up the pastry with your fingers to a height of 9–10cm. Place the pie mould in the fridge and chill until the pastry is firm enough to hold its shape. Lift off the wooden mould and return the pie shell to the fridge. Repeat to mould a second pie shell. Refrigerate for about an hour until both pie shells are firm.

illustrated on previous page

I've adored pork pies ever since I first came across them when I arrived in England. I can assure you that these taste far better than any you can buy! You will need a round wooden raised pie mould, about 10 cm diameter, 12 cm high.

Place the pastry shells on a baking sheet and spoon in enough pork filling to one-third fill each of them. Wrap the hard-boiled eggs in the bacon rashers and stand one egg upright in each pie. Fill up the pies with the remaining pork filling all round the egg and almost to the top of the crust. Leaving an even border extending 2 cm above the filling, cut off the excess pastry with scissors.

For the pie lids, divide the remaining 150g pastry in half and roll out each portion to a disc the same diameter as the pies. Brush the pie borders with eggwash, then position the pastry lids. Pinch each border between your thumb and index finger to seal it and form an attractive crest. Chill the pies for at least 2 hours.

To cook the pies, heat the oven to 180°C / Gas 4. Brush the surface of the pies with eggwash and cut a small aperture in the centre of each with a sharp knife. Bake in the oven for 35 minutes. To check the cooking, insert a trussing needle into the pies, taking care not to puncture the egg; the needle should come out hot. Using a palette knife, carefully lift the pies onto a wire rack and leave to cool for about 3 hours.

When the pies are cold, place greaseproof paper cones in the apertures and pour in the almost half-set jelly. Chill the pies for at least 24 hours before serving.

Serve the pies whole and cut into portions at the table. They are delicious with celeriac rémoulade or a salad of grated carrot tossed in vinaigrette with chopped mint.

venison, pheasant and pistachio pâté en croute

serves 12

950g raised pie pastry (see pages 164–5)	1/2 egg
1kg venison fillet, trimmed	100ml truffle juice
250g boned pheasant breasts, skinned and trimmed	5g flat leaf parsley, snipped
	5g salt
400g pork fat	3g freshly ground pepper
60g chicken livers	pinch of cayenne pepper
75ml Cognac	20g dried cranberries
100ml ruby port	20g pistachio nuts, skinned
200g double cream	250g thinly sliced pork fat, for barding
1 egg yolk	eggwash (1 egg yolk mixed with 1 tbsp milk)

For the filling, cut 250g of the venison into long strips, wrap in cling film and refrigerate. Cut the rest of the venison, the pheasant and pork fat into small strips. Place in a large bowl with the chicken livers, Cognac and port. Toss to mix, then cover with cling film and leave to marinate in the fridge for 12 hours.

For the jelly, preheat the oven to 200°C/Gas 6. Put the oil, venison bones and pheasant carcasses in a roasting pan and roast in the oven for about 20 minutes until lightly browned. Add the onion and carrot and cook for another 5 minutes. Deglaze with the port and tip everything into a saucepan. Pour in enough water to cover the bones, add the bouquet garni and orange zest, then bring to the boil. Lower the heat and cook gently for 1 hour, skimming the surface regularly. Pass the stock through a chinois, then boil to reduce by two-thirds. Season with salt and pepper and set aside.

Pass the chilled meat mixture through the coarse blade of a mincer and place in a bowl. Add the cream, egg yolk, egg, truffle juice, parsley, salt, pepper, cayenne, cranberries and pistachios, and mix thoroughly.

To assemble the pâté, on a lightly floured surface, roll out the pastry to a 30 x 20cm rectangle, 5mm thick. Trim the edges neatly using a sharp knife. Lay the strips of barding fat in the centre of the rectangle, along its length, so that they almost cover the pastry. Put the filling mixture in the centre, forming a sausage shape along four-fifths of the length of the pastry. Lay the strips of venison fillet randomly in the mixture. Fold the barding fat over the filling.

illustrated on previous page

This pâté will keep for up to a week in the fridge. Save the bones from the venison and the pheasant carcasses to make the jelly.

jelly
2 tbsp groundnut oil
500g venison bones and pheasant carcasses,
  chopped
1 onion, coarsely chopped
1 carrot, coarsely chopped
500 ml ruby port
bouquet garni
pared zest of 1 orange
salt and freshly ground pepper

Brush the 2 ends of the pastry with eggwash and fold one side of the pastry over the filling. Brush the pastry covering the filling and the ends with eggwash, and fold the second side of the pastry over the filling. Roll out the 2 ends of the pastry and trim each end to an 8 cm flap. Brush with eggwash and fold them over the pâté. Hold a baking sheet on the side of the pâté at 45° and tip it sharply to turn the pâté over onto the sheet. Refrigerate for at least an hour.

Heat the oven to 180°C/Gas 4. Brush the pâté all over with eggwash and mark out leaf shapes with a knife tip. Use a sharp knife to cut 2 small holes in the pastry and bake for 50 minutes. To test, insert a trussing needle into the centre of the pâté; it should be hot when you remove it. Use a palette knife to transfer the pâté to a wire rack and leave to cool for at least 4 hours.

Make 2 funnels of greaseproof paper, insert in the holes in the pastry and pour in the almost cold jelly. Refrigerate the pâté for at least 24 hours before serving.

Cut off the ends with a very sharp knife, then cut the pâté into neat slices and serve. Pickled walnuts and a simple watercress salad are ideal accompaniments.

chicken and chicken liver pâté en croûte

serves 20

600g raised pie pastry (see pages 164–5),
   not too cold
1.2 kg chicken thighs, boned, skinned and
   well chilled
200g pork fat, derinded, cut into long strips
   and well chilled
2 tbsp thyme sprigs
100 ml sweet white wine, preferably Sauternes
300 ml double cream
2 small (55g) eggs
2 egg yolks
6g salt

6g freshly ground pepper
2 tbsp runny honey
500g chicken breast fillets, skinned
120g butter
2 large pinches of cep powder
2 large onions, about 250g each, finely
   chopped
2 tbsp groundnut oil
400g chicken livers, trimmed and cut
   into large pieces
salt and freshly ground pepper
200g thinly sliced pork fat, for barding

For the filling, cut the chicken thighs into small pieces and put them in a bowl with the strips of pork fat and thyme sprigs. Moisten with the wine, cover with cling film and refrigerate for 12 hours.

The next day, pass the very cold meats through the coarse blade of a mincer and place in a bowl. Add the cream, eggs and yolks, salt, pepper and honey, and mix thoroughly.

Cut the chicken breast fillets into long strips. Heat half the butter in a frying pan and sear the chicken for 1 minute. Sprinkle on the cep powder and remove with a slotted spoon to a plate. Add the remaining butter to the frying pan and melt over a low heat, then add the onions. Sweat very gently for 20 minutes, stirring every 2 or 3 minutes until well cooked and lightly confit. Remove with a slotted spoon to a plate.

Heat the oil in a large frying pan, add the chicken livers and sear over a high heat for 20 seconds. Season with salt and pepper and place in a bowl.

To assemble the pâté, butter a rectangular hinged pie mould, 43 cm long, 10 cm wide and 8.5 cm deep. Roll out the pastry on a lightly floured surface to a rectangle, the same size as the mould. Generously dust the top with flour, lift up the pastry and work it with your fist to start to form a slight hollow. Turn the pastry over and drop it into the buttered mould. Use your fingertips to make the pastry adhere to the sides and base of the mould, and push it right into the corners and base, using a small piece of well-floured pastry to tamp it in.

Use scissors to cut off any excess pastry extending more than 1cm above the top of the mould, then pinch the edges to make an attractive crest. Refrigerate for 20 minutes.

Line the pastry with the thin slices of pork fat, then cover the side and bottom with a thin layer of onions. Spoon a 2 cm thick layer of filling in the mould, then arrange half the chicken breast strips and chicken livers on top. Cover with another layer of filling, make another layer of chicken breast and livers, then cover with the remaining filling. Fold the overhanging pork fat over the filling, and refrigerate the pâté for at least 2 hours.

To cook, preheat the oven to 180°C / Gas 4. Place the mould on a baking sheet and cook the pâté for 20 minutes, then lower the oven setting to 160°C / Gas 2$^{1}/_{2}$ and cook for another 40 minutes. To check the cooking, insert a trussing needle into the centre of the pâté; if it comes out hot, the pâté is done. Transfer it to a wire rack and leave to cool for 2 hours. Open the hinges and remove the sides of the mould. Leave the pâté to cool for another 2 hours (4 hours in all), then chill it for 24 hours.

To serve, cut the pâté into neat slices with a very sharp knife, discarding the end slices. A simple salad of mâche and pickled cherries or black olives are ideal partners.

This pâté is perfect for a buffet lunch. The onions act as a soft cushion between the crust and the filling, so jelly is not necessary.

I love the indulgence of a large luscious brioche. It must be light with doughy filaments — the colour of a perfect yellow egg yolk — and have a sweet, buttery aroma. It should taste rich but not sickly, and should leave no trace of butter on your fingers.

If you ever happen to visit Crans-Montana in Switzerland, try the large brioches at the Pâtisserie Taillens — they are superb. To make a really good brioche, you'll need to use very fresh free-range eggs and fine quality butter with a nutty flavour. The step-by-step instructions on the following pages will enable you to tackle this dough with confidence — it takes no more than 20 minutes using an electric mixer fitted with a dough hook.

This chapter also includes coulibiac dough, which is very similar to brioche but contains less butter. It is made in exactly the same way as brioche dough and is ideal for encasing fillets of salmon or sea bass as well as for beef en croûte. Do try it for these savoury dishes — it is seductively light and crisp.

brioche dough

brioche dough

makes about 1.2kg dough

This classic French dough can be frozen, well wrapped, for up to 2 weeks.

70ml tepid milk
15g fresh yeast
500g plain flour
15g fine salt
6 eggs
350g butter, slightly softened
30g caster sugar
eggwash (1 egg yolk mixed with 1 tbsp milk)

Put the milk and yeast into a bowl and stir to dissolve the yeast. Put the flour, salt and eggs in an electric mixer fitted with a dough hook and pour in the milk and yeast mixture. Mix on low speed to combine and knead the dough for 5 minutes.

Scrape down the sides of the bowl with a rubber spatula, then knead at medium speed for about 10 minutes. By this stage, the dough should be smooth, elastic and well amalgamated.

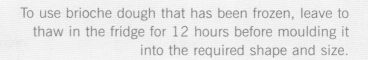

To use brioche dough that has been frozen, leave to thaw in the fridge for 12 hours before moulding it into the required shape and size.

Remove the dough hook, leaving the dough in the bowl. Cover with a tea towel or cling film and leave to rise at approximately 24°C for about 2 hours until the dough has doubled in volume.

Meanwhile, in another bowl, mix the butter and sugar together well. Add a few small pieces to the dough, then with the mixer running at low speed, add the rest, a piece a time. When the butter mixture is all incorporated, increase the speed and work for 6–10 minutes until the dough is very smooth and shiny, and comes away from the bowl with perfect elasticity.

Knock the dough back by flipping it over 2 or 3 times with your hand. Cover the bowl again and refrigerate for several hours (but not more than 24 hours). The dough is then ready to use and mould.

continued overleaf

shaping a large brioche

You will need a buttered brioche mould, measuring 16 cm across the top, 8 cm across the base.

Shape the small piece of dough into a ball and roll it at an angle into an elongated oval.

Divide 600g dough into two-thirds (400g) and one-third (200g). Shape the larger piece into a ball and place it in the bottom of the mould. Press 2 fingers into the centre of the dough to make a deep indentation.

Lightly flour your index and middle fingers, then gently press the narrow end of the oval into the indentation in the large ball, so that about two-thirds of the dough disappears into the base of the brioche and only a little is left visible, resembling a 'head'.

Lightly brush the 'head' and body of the dough with eggwash. Leave the brioche to rise at approximately 24°C for about 1^1/$_2$ hours until it has at least doubled in volume.

Preheat the oven to 200°C/Gas 6. Working from the outside inwards, brush the brioche very lightly with eggwash. Dip a pair of very sharp scissors into cold water and make six 3 cm deep cuts around the body of the dough. Immediately bake the brioche for 15 minutes, then lower the oven setting to 170°C/Gas 3 and bake for another 30 minutes. Leave the brioche in the mould for 5 minutes, then unmould it onto a wire rack and leave to cool.

baked brioche illustrated overleaf

Purists like to tear the brioche apart with their fingers, but it is easier to slice it with a serrated knife and pass it round for guests to help themselves.

shaping small brioche

You will need 20 buttered individual brioche moulds, measuring 8 cm across the top, 4 cm across the base (or 10 moulds if you bake the brioche in 2 batches). Use a 60g ball of dough for each one, roll it into an elongated egg shape and narrow one end by pressing and rolling it with the edge of your hand. Place the larger end in the bottom of the mould, then dip your index finger in flour and push the narrow end into the mass to leave a small 'head' protruding in the middle. Brush with eggwash and leave to rise for about 30 minutes, then bake at 180°C/Gas 4 for about 10 minutes. Transfer to a wire rack to cool.

serves 6

240g brioche dough (see pages 184–5)
12 thin streaky bacon rashers, derinded
eggwash (1 egg yolk mixed with 1 tbsp milk)

Divide the dough into 12 pieces, each about 20g. On a lightly floured surface, roll each piece into a sausage shape, about 15 cm long. Tightly roll a bacon rasher in a spiral around each 'brioche sausage' and put the twists on a baking sheet, spacing them about 4 cm apart. Leave in a warm place (20–24°C) for 30 minutes until risen.

Preheat the oven to 180°C / Gas 4. Delicately brush the brioche with eggwash, taking care not to glaze the bacon. Bake the twists for 12 minutes, then immediately transfer them to a wire rack with a palette knife. The brioche twists are best served straight away. Pile them onto plates and let everyone help themselves.

These twists are perfect for breakfast or a Sunday brunch treat. I love to eat them with scrambled eggs, as they are so much more interesting than toast.

mousseline brioche canapés

serves 8

360g brioche dough (see pages 184–5)
eggwash (1 egg yolk mixed with 1 tbsp milk)

toppings
1 tbsp strong mustard
140g butter, softened
16 thin slices pancetta
16 thin slices chorizo sausage

8 caper berries
2 avocados
juice of $1/2$ lemon
8 prawns, cooked and peeled (tails left on)
4 tbsp mayonnaise (see page 288)
8 asparagus tips, thinly sliced lengthways,
     blanched for 10 seconds and drained
1 tbsp grated horseradish

Butter the inside of a mousseline brioche mould or small ovenproof saucepan (ideally copper), 10 cm in diameter and 8 cm deep. Then line it with generously buttered greaseproof paper to extend 10 cm above the top of the mould. Secure the protruding paper cylinder with 2 staples or kitchen string.

On a lightly floured surface, shape the brioche dough into a ball, put it into the mould and press down lightly with your fist. Leave to rise at 24°C for about $2^{1}/2$ hours until it has tripled in volume.

Preheat the oven to 170°C/Gas 3. Brush the top of the brioche with eggwash. Dip the blades of very sharp scissors in cold water and make five 3 cm deep cuts in the top. Immediately bake the brioche for 35 minutes. Leave it in the mould for 5 minutes, then unmould it without removing the greaseproof paper and place on a wire rack. Leave until almost cold before peeling off the paper. The brioche is ready to use as soon as it is completely cold.

To assemble and serve Lay the brioche on its side on a breadboard and slice into about 16 rounds, 6 mm thick, using a serrated knife. Cut each round in half.

Pancetta and chorizo canapés Mix the mustard with 40g softened butter and spread over 8 half-rounds of brioche. Arrange 2 slices each of pancetta and chorizo on each brioche base and garnish with a caper berry.

illustrated on previous page

8 small thin slices smoked salmon
6 cherry tomatoes, quartered
8 chervil sprigs
sea salt flakes
freshly ground pepper
12 red radishes, some thinly sliced,
   some cut into matchsticks, some
   finely diced

Avocado and prawn canapés Halve the avocados, prise out the stone and scoop the flesh into balls (about 32 in total), using a small melon baller. Toss them with the lemon juice. Cut the prawns along three-quarters of their length, and arrange one on each of 8 brioche halves. Coat generously with mayonnaise and put 2 avocado balls on each side of the prawn. Roll up the asparagus slices and place two on each canapé.

Smoked salmon and tomato canapés Mix the horseradish with 30g softened butter. Spread the mixture onto 8 brioche halves. Drape a slice of smoked salmon on each and garnish with some cherry tomato wedges and a sprig of chervil.

Radish canapés Spread 70g softened butter onto 8 brioche halves. Season with a few flakes of salt and a grinding of pepper, then arrange the radishes as you wish.

Serve the canapés on a large platter, with aperitifs or for Sunday brunch.

You can vary the toppings of these tempting canapés according to the season. The mousseline brioche bases have a surprising delicacy. Assemble them just before serving to preserve their freshness.

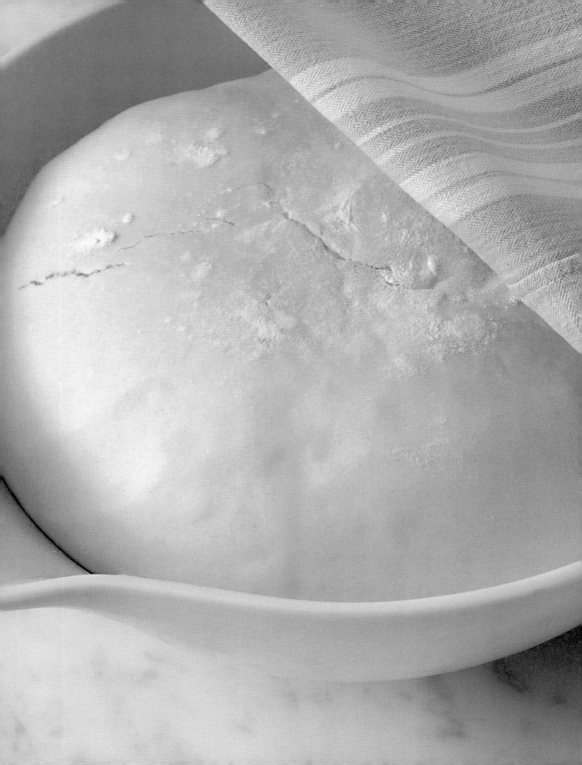

salmon coulibiac

serves 8

Enveloped in pastry with rice, mushrooms and onions, the salmon remains wonderfully moist.

pastry
260 ml tepid milk
12 g fresh yeast
450 g plain flour
10 g fine salt
3 egg yolks
90 g butter, slightly softened
45 g caster sugar
eggwash (1 egg yolk mixed with 1 tbsp milk)

filling
120 g clarified butter (see page 297)
1 middle cut of salmon, about 1.3 kg,
  filleted and skinned
salt and freshly ground pepper
160 g butter
3 shallots, finely chopped
60 g white rice
small bouquet garni

Make the coulibiac pastry following the step-by-step instructions for brioche dough (on pages 184–5), adding the ingredients listed above in the same order as for brioche. (The resulting dough will be firmer and less rich.) Leave to rise and rest in the fridge as for brioche.

For the salmon, heat half the clarified butter in a large frying pan. Season one salmon fillet with salt and pepper and sear over a high heat for 2–3 minutes on each side until lightly golden on both sides, then lift onto a plate. Add the remaining clarified butter to the pan, season the second salmon fillet and sear in the same way, then remove to a plate. Leave the fillets to cool, then cover with cling film and refrigerate.

For the rice, preheat the oven to 180°C/Gas 4. Heat 40 g butter in a small deep ovenproof frying pan and gently sweat one-third of the shallots until soft. Add the rice, 100 ml water, the bouquet garni, saffron and a pinch of salt, put the lid on and cook in the oven for 16 minutes. Tip the rice into a bowl, discarding the bouquet garni, and leave to cool, then refrigerate.

For the mushrooms, heat 60 g of the butter in a pan over a medium heat. Add the chopped mushrooms and lemon juice and cook, stirring from time to time, until all the moisture has evaporated. Add the remaining shallots and half the cream and cook until the cream is absorbed. Season to taste and leave to cool, then refrigerate.

For the onions, heat 60 g butter in a pan over a medium heat, add the onions and cook gently for 10 minutes, stirring occasionally. Add the rest of the cream and cook gently for another 10 minutes. Season, leave to cool, then refrigerate.

illustrated on pages 194 – 5

10 saffron strands
250 g button mushrooms, finely chopped
juice of 1 lemon
180 ml double cream
250 g onions, finely chopped
4 herb crêpes (see page 290)
2 hard-boiled eggs, coarsely chopped
2 tbsp snipped flat leaf parsley

To assemble the coulibiac, on a lightly floured surface, roll out the pastry to a 40 x 30 cm rectangle, 3 mm thick. Trim the sides to neaten. Place 2 herb crêpes along the middle of the rectangle. Spoon half the mushrooms on top and spread along the length of the crêpes.

Put one salmon fillet on the mushrooms and cover it with the onions, chopped hard-boiled egg and parsley. Place the second fillet on top, spread with the rest of the mushrooms and then cover with the rice. Lay the remaining 2 crêpes over the top. Fold them over the salmon and if necessary cut off any overlapping parts with scissors. Lightly brush the 2 ends of the pastry rectangle with eggwash. Fold one side over the salmon, brush it and the ends with eggwash, then fold the other side over.

Roll out the 2 ends of the pastry to a 5 – 6 mm thickness and trim to an 8 cm length. Brush these with eggwash and fold them over the salmon. Turn the coulibiac over onto a baking sheet and refrigerate for 30 minutes. Meanwhile, heat the oven to 180°C / Gas 4.

Brush the entire surface of the coulibiac with eggwash and score it with leaf patterns using the tip of a small, sharp knife. Cut a small aperture in the middle of the pastry to allow the steam to escape during cooking. Bake the coulibiac for 35 minutes if you like your salmon quite rare, or 45 minutes for medium. Use a palette knife to transfer it to a wire rack.

Leave to rest for 5 minutes, then cut the coulibiac into 1.5 cm thick slices and serve at once on individual plates. I like to serve it with a salad of thinly sliced raw fennel dressed with a few chervil leaves, lemon juice and a drizzle of light olive oil.

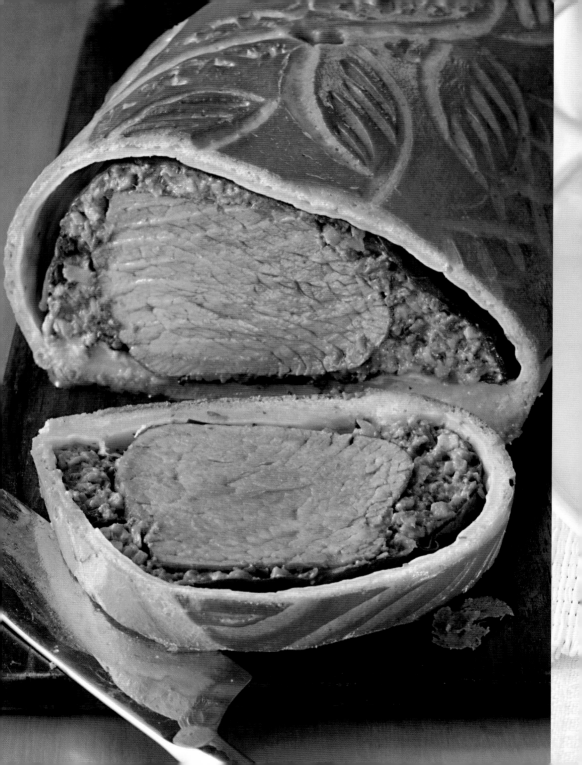

fillet of beef in a pastry crust

serves 6

pastry
260 ml tepid milk
12 g fresh yeast
450 g plain flour
10 g fine salt
3 egg yolks
90 g butter, slightly softened
45 g caster sugar

filling
1 fillet of beef, about 800 g–1 kg, cut from the thicker end
salt and freshly ground pepper
80 g clarified butter (see page 297)
60 g butter
500 g button mushrooms, finely chopped
juice of 1 lemon

Make the pastry following the step-by-step instructions for brioche dough (on pages 184–5), adding the ingredients listed above in the same order as for brioche. The resulting dough is firmer and less rich than brioche, and is perfect for beef en croûte. Leave the dough to rise and rest in the fridge exactly as for brioche.

For the beef fillet, preheat the oven to 200°C/Gas 6. Trim the fillet of any membrane, then season all over with salt and pepper. Heat the clarified butter in a roasting pan over a medium-high heat and sear the beef for 3–4 minutes until golden, turning to colour evenly. Transfer to the oven and roast for 6 minutes, turning the meat over after 3 minutes. Lift the beef onto a wire rack and leave to cool completely. At this stage, it will be very rare.

For the mushroom duxelles, heat the 60 g butter in a pan over a medium heat. Add the mushrooms and lemon juice and cook, stirring from time to time, until all the moisture has evaporated. Add the shallot and cook for another 2 minutes, then pour in the cream and cook, stirring, until it is all absorbed. Season to taste and set aside to cool, then chill.

Blanch the spinach leaves in boiling salted water for 30 seconds, then drain and refresh in cold water. Drain well, separate the leaves and pat each one dry with kitchen paper.

To assemble, roll out the pastry on a lightly floured surface to a 40 x 25 cm rectangle, 3–4 mm thick. Trim the sides to neaten. Place 2 crêpes along the middle of the rectangle and cover them with 8 spinach leaves. Spoon and spread a 1 cm thick band of mushroom

The beef can be wrapped in its pastry crust up to 4 hours in advance and kept in the fridge – ready to bake when you are ready to eat…

60g shallot, finely chopped
100 ml double cream
12 large spinach leaves
4 herb crêpes (see page 290)
eggwash (1 egg yolk mixed with 1 tbsp milk)

to serve
béarnaise sauce (see page 287)

duxelles along the middle of the spinach and crêpes. Put the cold beef fillet on top and thickly cover the whole surface, including the ends, with the remaining duxelles.

Cover the mushroom duxelles with the remaining spinach leaves and crêpes. Fold the crêpes over the beef and if necessary cut off any overlapping parts with scissors. Lightly brush the 2 ends of the pastry rectangle with eggwash. Fold one side over the beef, brush it and the ends with eggwash, then fold the other side over the beef.

Roll out the 2 ends of the pastry to a 5–6mm thickness, and trim to an 8cm length. Brush these with eggwash and fold them over the beef. Turn the pastry-wrapped beef over onto a baking sheet and refrigerate for 30 minutes. Meanwhile, heat the oven to 200°C/Gas 6.

Brush the entire surface of the pastry with eggwash and score it with leaf patterns using a knife tip. Cut a small aperture in the middle of the pastry to allow the steam to escape during cooking. Bake for 25 minutes if you like your beef rare, or 35 minutes for medium. If the pastry becomes too brown as it cooks, cover loosely with foil and lower the oven setting to 170°C/Gas 3.

Use a palette knife to transfer the cooked beef en croûte to a wire rack and leave it to rest for 5 minutes. Carve the beef in its crust into thick slices and serve on warm plates, with a generous spoonful of béarnaise sauce. I like to accompany this dish with semi-confit cherry tomatoes (page 289) and steamed broccoli.

st-genix brioches with pink pralines

serves 8–10

The town of St-Genix is famous for its Pompadour pink pralines,
which flavour and colour these brioches.

350g brioche dough (see pages 184–5)
20 pink pralines (pink-tinted sugar coated
   almonds)
eggwash (1 egg yolk mixed with 1 tbsp milk)

On a lightly floured surface, push the brioche dough 2 or 3 times with the palm of
your hand to make it supple and malleable. Scatter the pink pralines over the dough and
gently knead them in, taking care to avoid overworking the dough.

Shape the dough into a ball, put it on a lightly floured baking sheet and place a 20 cm
diameter, 2 cm deep pastry ring around it. Roll the dough with a rolling pin until it
fills the ring, then remove the ring. Leave to rise at about 25°C for an hour.

Preheat the oven to 180°C/Gas 4. Brush the top of the brioche very lightly with eggwash
and bake in the oven for 35 minutes. Use a palette knife to transfer it to a wire rack and
leave to cool before serving.

Perfect for breakfast – or with coffee at any time – these lovely brioches are
best eaten as soon as they have cooled, while the pralines are still crunchy.

makes 12

12 small brioches (see page 188)
200 ml sugar syrup (see page 291)
50 ml kirsch
240g mixed crystallised fruits (cherries,
  orange peel, angelica), finely diced

60g raisins, blanched for 2 minutes,
  refreshed and well drained
480g crème pâtissière (see page 292)
400g Italian meringue (see page 294)
80g flaked almonds, very lightly toasted

Preheat the oven to 180°C/Gas 4. Using a serrated knife, cut off the tops of the brioches and set aside. Using a small knife, carefully take out the insides, leaving a 1cm thick shell all round and at the base. Mix the sugar syrup and kirsch together, then lightly brush the mixture over the inside of the brioche shells and onto the underside of the tops.

Mix the crystallised fruits and raisins into the crème pâtissière. Spoon the mixture into the brioche shells and replace the tops.

Use a palette knife to spread the meringue in a 5–7mm layer over the top half of the brioches, sprinkle on the toasted almonds and arrange the brioches on a baking sheet. Bake for 4–5 minutes until the meringue forms a light crust. Remove from the oven before the meringue starts to crack or colour. Use a palette knife to transfer the brioches to a wire rack and leave to cool before serving.

A Parisian patissier came up with the idea for these individual kirsch-soaked brioches as a way of using up unsold small brioches. They taste as good as they look…

rum babas with chantilly cream

makes 24

baba dough
65 ml tepid milk
30g fresh yeast
500g plain flour
10g fine salt
8 eggs
125g butter, melted, cooled and mixed with 45g caster sugar

to serve
2 litres heavy sugar syrup (see page 291, made with 750g sugar)
300ml dark rum (preferably Captain Morgan)
460g chantilly cream (see page 295)
24 mint sprigs
24 raspberries

You will need 24 lightly buttered baba moulds, 7.5 cm diameter, 1.5 cm deep (or 8 or 12 moulds if making the babas in batches). Make the baba dough following the brioche dough instructions (on pages 184–5), adding the ingredients listed above in the same order as for brioche. Once you've incorporated the melted butter and sugar mix, knead the dough for no more than 5 minutes; it will be very soft. Leave to rise and rest in the fridge as for brioche.

To shape the babas, take a small ball of the dough and place in a mould. With the heel of your hand, spread it evenly up to the edge of the mould, but not above it. Repeat with the rest. Place on a baking sheet and leave at 24°C for 45 minutes until doubled in volume.

Preheat the oven to 180°C/Gas 4. Cook the babas for 18–20 minutes, then immediately unmould onto a wire rack, rounded side down. Heat the sugar syrup in a wide shallow saucepan to 60°C. Soak the babas 8 at a time. Place in the syrup, rounded sides down, for 10 minutes, then turn carefully, with a small slotted spoon and soak for another 6–8 minutes. Press with your finger to check that they are thoroughly soaked; they should feel tender and pliable. Place rounded side down on a wire rack over a dish to catch the syrup as it drains. (You'll need to thin the syrup with 150–200ml boiling water before soaking the final batch if it has become too thick and sweet.)

When the babas are cold, douse them with half the rum, leave them for 5 minutes, then douse them again with the rest. Using a piping bag fitted with a 1cm fluted nozzle, fill the centre of each baba generously with a rosette of chantilly cream. Decorate with a mint sprig and a halved raspberry to serve.

This is one of my favourite desserts. It is difficult to make a smaller quantity of dough, but you can freeze any cooked babas that are not needed straight away for up to 2 weeks. Thaw them for 2–3 hours before soaking in syrup.

Croissant dough is somewhat akin to puff pastry, in so far as a slab of butter is incorporated into the basic mixture and the dough is rolled and 'turned', but it actually belongs to the family of yeasted doughs, like brioche.

Naturally, the dough is most often shaped into croissants, which are universally popular, but it can also be used for pains aux raisins and pains au chocolat. I like to concoct mini savoury croissants with ham, tapenade, grated Comté cheese and the like — to serve as cocktail canapés. They are always the first to disappear from the platter.

For me, it is always a magical moment each morning around 7 am at The Waterside Inn, when our tourier Douglas starts baking the croissants. The wonderful aroma from the oven gently pervades the corridors and sleeping guests share the magic. They tell me it's like awakening from a dream that's good enough to eat…

croissant dough

croissant dough

This classic dough is used to make various sweet and savoury pastries. You can freeze uncooked croissants and pains au chocolat after shaping (before brushing with eggwash) for up to 2 weeks. Arrange interleaved with greaseproof paper in suitable containers, so you can take out as many as you wish.

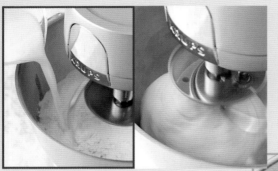

Cover the bowl with cling film and leave the dough to rise in a warm place (at about 24°C) until doubled in volume; this should take 45 minutes – 1 hour. Knock back the dough by flipping it over with your hand to release the carbon gas, but do not overwork it. Cover the bowl again with cling film and place in the fridge for at least 4 hours, but not more than 8 hours. Knock back the dough in the bowl again, then transfer it to a lightly floured work surface.

25g fresh yeast
250ml whole milk
500g plain flour
12g fine salt
50g caster sugar
275g butter, cold but not too hard
eggwash (1 egg yolk mixed with 1 tbsp milk)

Dissolve the yeast in the milk in a bowl. Put the flour, salt and sugar in an electric mixer fitted with a dough hook and mix at low speed, gradually adding the yeast mixture. Stop working the dough as soon as it comes away from the sides of the bowl; the texture must not become too elastic.

Shape the dough into a ball and cut a 3 cm deep cross in the centre. Roll out the 4 sides to make flaps. Bash the butter into a rectangle with the rolling pin and place it in the centre. Fold the flaps over the butter to envelop it completely.

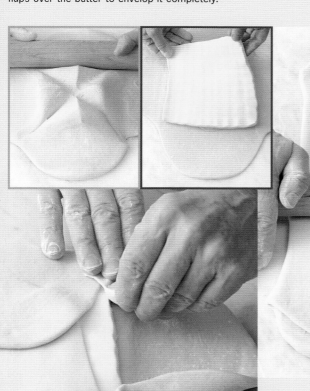

First turn Lightly flouring the surface as necessary, roll the dough out to a 60 x 30 cm rectangle. Fold in three. Wrap in cling film and chill for 30 minutes.
Second turn Give the chilled dough a quarter-turn, roll out to a rectangle, fold again, wrap and chill as above.
Third and final turn Roll the dough out in the opposite direction from the previous turn to a rectangle and fold as before. Wrap in cling film and chill for at least 30 minutes (no more than 1 hour).

continued overleaf

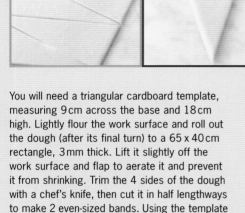

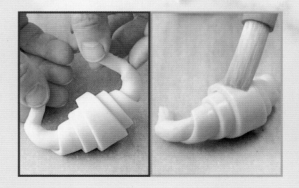

You will need a triangular cardboard template, measuring 9 cm across the base and 18 cm high. Lightly flour the work surface and roll out the dough (after its final turn) to a 65 x 40 cm rectangle, 3 mm thick. Lift it slightly off the work surface and flap to aerate it and prevent it from shrinking. Trim the 4 sides of the dough with a chef's knife, then cut it in half lengthways to make 2 even-sized bands. Using the template as a guide, cut the dough into triangles.

Lay a dough triangle on the work surface with the base towards you. Use the knife to make a 1 cm deep incision in the middle of the base, pull the 2 points of the base slightly, then pull the point of the triangle.

Roll up the triangle from the base to the point. (For a savoury croissant, lay a slice of ham at the base before starting to roll.) Immediately place on a baking sheet and turn the points inwards to make a crescent. Repeat to make the other croissants as quickly as possible.

Lightly brush the croissants with eggwash, starting on the inside and working outwards, so that the layers of dough do not stick together and prevent the croissants from rising properly.

Put the baking sheets in a warm, preferably slightly humid place (at 24 – 30°C) and leave the croissants to rise for 2 hours until they have almost doubled in size. When they are nearly ready, preheat the oven to 170°C/Gas 3. Lightly brush the croissants with eggwash again and bake for 12 – 14 minutes.

Pains au chocolat are lovely served while still slightly warm from the oven, with the chocolate soft and melting in the centre. Similarly pains aux raisins are best eaten on the day you make them.

pains au chocolat

makes 20 – 22

These can be frozen in the same way as croissants (see page 210).
After thawing, warm through gently in the oven to serve.

**1.1 kg croissant dough, prepared with 3 turns
  (see pages 210 – 11)**
40 – 44 sticks of dark chocolate, 4g each
eggwash (1 egg yolk mixed with 1 tbsp milk)

On a lightly floured surface, roll the dough into a rectangle about 52 x 46 cm, 5 mm thick. Trim the edges with a chef's knife, then cut the rectangle lengthways into 4 long bands, about 11 cm wide. Cut across each band every 7 cm to make 11 x 7 cm rectangles.

Lay one of the small rectangles of dough in front of you, with a shorter edge facing you. Lay a stick of chocolate across the rectangle, 4 cm in from the top edge. Fold the top 4 cm of dough over the chocolate, then place a second stick of chocolate next to the cut edge. Roll the dough over again to enclose the chocolate. Transfer the pain au chocolat to a baking sheet. Shape the rest in the same way, then brush lightly with eggwash.

Put the baking sheets of croissants in a warm, preferably slightly humid place at 24 – 30°C and leave to rise for 2 hours until they have almost doubled in size. Preheat the oven to 170°C / Gas 3.

To bake, brush the croissants very lightly again with eggwash and bake for 12 minutes. Transfer them immediately to a wire rack, taking care that they are not touching, and leave to cool for a while before serving.

illustrated with pains aux raisins on previous page

makes 30

1.1 kg croissant dough, prepared with 3 turns
  (see pages 210–11)
400g crème pâtissière made substituting half
  the flour with custard powder (see page 292)
eggwash (1 egg yolk mixed with 1 tbsp milk)

sultanas
250g sultanas
100g caster sugar
50 ml dark rum (preferably Negrita or
  Captain Morgan's), optional

For the sultanas, put 200 ml water in a saucepan and add the sugar, sultanas and rum if using. Slowly bring to the boil over a low heat and let bubble gently for 2 minutes. Remove from the heat and leave to stand for 2 hours. Drain the sultanas thoroughly just before using.

On a lightly floured surface, roll the dough into a rectangle about 65 x 35 cm, 4 mm thick. Trim the edges with a chef's knife, then use a palette knife to spread the crème pâtissière evenly over the dough, leaving a 1 cm margin free all round. Scatter the sultanas over the crème pâtissière and brush the pastry edges with eggwash.

Working away from you, roll the pastry rectangle into a sausage shape. Place on a baking sheet and put in the freezer for 30–45 minutes.

Using a very sharp knife, cut the pastry sausage into 2 cm thick rounds and place them, cut side down on a baking sheet. Leave in a warm place (at 24–30°C) for 1 hour. Preheat the oven to 170°C/Gas 3.

Bake the pains aux raisins for 12 minutes, then transfer them immediately to a wire rack with a palette knife. Leave to cool until just warm before serving.

croissant baguette with pesto

serves 6–8

**480g croissant dough, prepared with 3 turns
(see pages 210–11)
eggwash (1 egg yolk mixed with 1 tbsp milk)
100g pesto (see page 288, or use ready-made)
10g pine nuts**

On a lightly floured surface, roll the croissant dough into a 40 x 20cm rectangle, 4mm thick. Lay the rectangle on a sheet of greaseproof paper, with a longer side facing you. Trim the sides with a chef's knife to neaten. Brush a 4cm border along the shorter sides of the dough with eggwash, and a 5cm border on the longer side furthest from you.

Spoon the pesto all over the unglazed dough. Starting from the long edge nearest to you, and using the greaseproof paper to help, lift the dough and roll it into an even sausage shape to form the baguette. Still using the greaseproof paper, roll the baguette onto a baking sheet. Leave it in a warm place (20–24°C) to rise for 45 minutes to an hour.

Preheat the oven to 180°C/Gas 4. Brush the top of the baguette with eggwash, then, using a very sharp knife, make eight 1cm deep incisions on the diagonal along the length of the baguette. Scatter the pine nuts over the top and bake for 20 minutes. Lower the oven setting to 160°C/Gas 2 1/2 and bake for another 15 minutes.

Leave the baguette on the baking sheet for 15 minutes, then use a palette knife to slide it onto a wooden board. Present the baguette whole at the table and carefully cut it into thick slices with a serrated knife. It is very fragile and is best served warm.

This light, airy, irresistible flaky baguette is particularly good served with
a bowl of fish soup. You can make a smaller version if you prefer.

Whatever their size, shape and flavour — coffee, caramel or chocolate — choux puffs and éclairs are high on everyone's list of favourite desserts, children and adults alike. As for me, I've always been torn between profiteroles filled with luscious vanilla ice cream and topped with lashings of chocolate sauce, and a grandiose St Honoré with chantilly cream — a dilemma I have never managed to resolve.

Choux paste is simplicity itself to make and allows you to create enticing sweet and savoury dishes. The aroma of the steam that drifts out of the oven as the choux puffs cook is gentle and inviting, and it's fascinating to see the puffs almost triple in volume. Once cooked, they should be firm and crisp on the surface and base, while the inside should stay soft and moist. The puffs can be cooked several hours in advance, but for best results, fill them just before serving.

choux pastry

choux paste

125 ml milk
125ml water
100g butter, diced
$^{1}/_{2}$ tsp salt
1 tsp caster sugar
150g plain flour
4 eggs
eggwash (1 egg yolk mixed with 1 tbsp milk)

Combine the milk, water, butter, salt and sugar in a saucepan and set over a low heat. Bring to the boil and immediately take the pan off the heat. Shower in the flour and mix with a wooden spoon until completely smooth.

Return the pan to a medium heat and stir continuously for about 1 minute to dry out the paste, then tip it into a bowl.

Add the eggs one at a time, beating with the wooden spoon.

Once the eggs are all incorporated, the paste should be smooth and shiny with a thick ribbon consistency. It is now ready to use. (If you're not using it immediately, brush the surface lightly with a little beaten egg to prevent a crust forming.)

You can easily adapt this recipe to make savoury choux, by adding a little cayenne or paprika.

continued overleaf

small choux buns

For small choux buns, put the paste into a piping bag fitted with a 1cm plain nozzle. Pipe small mounds in staggered rows onto a baking sheet lined with greaseproof paper for preference, or directly onto a greased baking sheet. Brush the choux with eggwash and lightly mark the tops with the back of a fork. Bake at 180°C/Gas 4 for 15–20 minutes until the outside of the buns is dry and crisp but the inside is still soft. Cool on a wire rack.

serves 10 (4 profiteroles per person)

1 quantity freshly made choux paste
  (see pages 222–3)
eggwash (1 egg yolk mixed with 1 tbsp milk)

filling
1 quantity vanilla ice cream, or $\frac{1}{2}$ quantity
  vanilla and $\frac{1}{2}$ quantity coffee ice cream
  (see page 293)

chocolate sauce
250g good-quality dark bitter chocolate,
  70% cocoa solids (preferably Valrhona)
200ml milk
3 tbsp double cream
40g caster sugar
30g butter, diced

Preheat the oven to 180°C / Gas 4. Line a baking sheet with greaseproof paper. Put the choux paste into a piping bag fitted with a 1 cm plain nozzle and pipe out about 40 puffs, 3 cm in diameter, following the instructions (see left). Brush with eggwash and bake in the oven for 20 minutes until dry and crisp on the outside, but still soft inside. As soon as they are cooked, transfer them to a wire rack and leave until cold. Using a serrated knife, cut across the top one-fifth of each puff, leaving a 'hinge' to make a lid. Set the puffs aside.

To make the chocolate sauce, chop the chocolate and place in a heatproof bowl over a pan of hot water to melt gently, stirring occasionally with a wooden spoon. Put the milk, cream and sugar into a saucepan and bring to the boil, whisking continuously. Take off the heat. Still whisking, pour on the melted chocolate, then return to the heat. Still whisking, let the sauce bubble briefly over a medium heat. Turn off the heat and whisk in the pieces of butter, one at a time. Pass the sauce through a fine chinois into a bowl, cover with cling film and keep warm in a bain-marie.

Generously fill the choux puffs with ice cream (if using both coffee and vanilla ice creams fill half the puffs with each), then re-position the lids. Serve in glass dishes. Pour on some of the chocolate sauce and serve the profiteroles immediately, handing the rest of the sauce around in a jug.

One of the delights of this luscious dessert is that all the elements
can be prepared a few hours in advance.

meteorite choux topped with sugar crystals

makes 32 (to serve 8)

1 quantity freshly made choux paste
  (see pages 222–3), still warm
100g whole almonds, skinned
eggwash (1 egg yolk mixed with 1 tbsp milk)
80g sugar nibs

Preheat the oven to 170°C/Gas 3. Scatter the almonds on a baking sheet and place in the oven for about 20 minutes, until dry and very pale golden. Tip onto a plate, leave to cool, then cut each one into 3 or 4 pieces. Increase the oven setting to 180°C/Gas 4.

Mix the almond pieces into the warm choux paste, then spoon it into a piping bag fitted with a 2cm plain nozzle. Line a baking sheet with greaseproof paper. Following the instructions on page 224, pipe out 32 choux mounds, 4cm in diameter, spacing them 4cm apart. Brush them very lightly with eggwash, but don't press with the back of a fork; instead, sprinkle them with sugar nibs.

Bake the choux for 15 minutes, then lower the oven setting to 170°C/Gas 3 and bake for another 15 minutes until golden and crisp. Transfer to a wire rack with a palette knife and allow to cool.

Serve the little choux buns on the day you bake them, with coffee, as a teatime treat or with a glass of dessert wine.

The way these choux buns become slightly misshapen as they cook so they resemble meteorites is intriguing. The inclusion of almonds makes them less airy than other choux, but gives a lovely crunchy texture.

makes 24 (to serve 8)

Be generous with the caramel topping for these chocolate cream-filled choux, allowing it to drizzle over the sides.

**1 quantity freshly made choux paste
  (see pages 222–3), still warm**
300g caster sugar
24 crystallised violets
500g chocolate crème pâtissière (see page 292)
200ml chantilly cream (see page 295)

Preheat the oven to 180°C/Gas 4. Line a baking sheet with greaseproof paper. Put the choux paste into a piping bag fitted with a 1.5cm plain nozzle and pipe 24 roughly pear-shaped choux, 4cm wide at the start and extending to 6cm long, in staggered rows.

Bake the salammbos for 25 minutes until crisp and dry on the outside and base, but still soft inside. Transfer to a wire rack and leave until cold. Carefully cut a small hole in the bases with a knife tip.

For the caramel, put 50ml water and the sugar into a heavy-based saucepan and slowly bring to the boil, skimming the surface as it begins to bubble. Dip a very clean pastry brush into cold water and brush down the inside of the pan near the boiling sugar to prevent it crystallising. When the temperature reaches 160°C and the sugar has almost caramelised, lower the heat and cook to a pale amber caramel. Immediately plunge the base of the pan into cold water for 10 seconds to stop further cooking. One at a time, dip the top of the salammbos into the caramel to coat thickly, then invert onto a baking sheet. Immediately place a crystallised violet on top of each one before the caramel sets.

To fill the salammbos, mix the chocolate crème pâtissière into the chantilly cream lightly with a whisk, without overworking. Put it into a piping bag fitted with a 1cm plain nozzle and pipe it into the salammbos through the holes in the base.

Serve 3 salammbos per person on individual plates, or arrange on a platter for everyone to help themselves.

roasted peaches on choux crowns

serves 4

This is a lovely way to serve fresh peaches at the height of their season. For the best flavour, use perfectly ripe fruit.

4 ripe medium yellow or white peaches
$1/2$ quantity freshly made choux paste
   (see pages 222–3)
eggwash (1 egg mixed with 1 tbsp milk)
25g flaked almonds
75g caster sugar
100g butter
1 tbsp grenadine syrup (optional)
juice of 1 lemon
icing sugar, to dust

To peel the peaches, lightly run the tip of a knife around the circumference, then immerse in a pan of boiling water. As soon as the skin starts to lift along the incision, take out the peaches and refresh in a bowl of iced water. Remove and pull off the skin. Put the peaches in a roasting dish, cover and leave to cool.

Preheat the oven to 200°C/Gas 6. Put the choux paste into a piping bag fitted with a 7mm plain nozzle. Pipe 4 discs, 6–7cm diameter (depending on the size of the fruit) onto a lightly greased baking sheet. Brush with eggwash and sprinkle with the almonds. Bake for about 20 minutes, propping the oven door slightly ajar halfway through cooking to allow the steam to escape – so that the choux becomes crisp on the outside. Transfer to a wire rack. Increase the oven setting to 220°C/Gas 7.

To roast the peaches, melt the sugar and butter in a small pan and cook gently, stirring with a wooden spatula, to make a very pale caramel. Carefully add the grenadine syrup if using, and the lemon juice. Still stirring, let bubble gently for 5 minutes. Spoon the caramel over the peaches and roast in the oven for about 10 minutes, basting them every 3 or 4 minutes (allow an extra 5 minutes roasting if the peaches are not very ripe). Leave to cool completely, basting every 10 minutes with the caramel until the peaches are cold.

Put the choux crowns on individual plates. Using a palette knife, place a roasted peach in the middle of each crown and dust with a veil of icing sugar. Spoon a little caramel over the peaches and serve the rest separately in a small jug.

gâteau st. honoré with cocoa-dusted chantilly cream

serves 8

200g puff pastry, either rough puff (see pages
  112–3) or classic (see pages 108–11)
1 quantity freshly made choux paste (see
  pages 222–3)
eggwash (1 egg yolk mixed 1 tbsp milk)

filling
600g chantilly cream flavoured generously
  with vanilla (see page 295)
2 tbsp unsweetened cocoa powder

caramel
200g caster sugar

For the pastry base, on a lightly floured surface roll out the puff pastry to a 24 cm diameter disc, 2 mm thick. Roll it loosely over the rolling pin and unroll it onto a baking sheet lightly moistened with cold water. Lay a 22 cm diameter flan ring on the pastry and cut off the excess pastry around the ring with a knife tip. Prick the base in about 10 places with a fork and refrigerate for 20 minutes. Preheat the oven to 180°C/Gas 4.

For the choux base, put a little less than two-thirds of the choux paste into a piping bag fitted with a 1 cm plain nozzle. Starting from the centre of the pastry base and working outwards, pipe a spiral, holding the nozzle 2 mm above the pastry and stopping 3 cm from the edge of the pastry to leave a clear border. Brush the border with eggwash, then pipe a 'crown' of choux paste onto the border, holding the nozzle at least 5 cm above the pastry. Brush the crown with eggwash and bake in the oven for 35 minutes. As soon as it is cooked, slide it onto a wire rack with the aid of a palette knife.

For the choux puffs, put the rest of the choux paste into a piping bag fitted with a 5 mm plain nozzle and pipe 16 puffs, 2 cm in diameter, onto a lightly greased baking sheet. Brush with eggwash and press the tops lightly with the back of a fork. Bake in the oven for 20 minutes. Carefully make a small hole in the base of each puff with a knife tip, then place on a wire rack.

illustrated on previous page

To make the caramel, put 50 ml water and the sugar into a small heavy-based saucepan and slowly bring to the boil. Dip a very clean pastry brush into cold water and brush down the inside of the pan near the boiling sugar to prevent it from crystallising as it caramelises. When the temperature reaches 160°C, lower the heat and cook to a pale amber caramel.

Spear the base of one choux puff with a knife tip, dip the top into the caramel to coat, then stand the puff on a chilled baking sheet. Repeat to coat the tops of the other 15 puffs. Leave until completely cold.

To assemble the St. Honoré, put a fifth of the chantilly cream into a piping bag fitted with a 5 mm plain nozzle and pipe it into the puffs through the holes in the bases. Arrange the puffs all round the edge of the choux pastry crown, attaching them firmly with a dab of caramel.

Put the rest of the chantilly cream into a piping bag fitted with a St-Honoré nozzle if you have one (otherwise simply use a large fluted nozzle). Pipe the cream attractively and generously into the centre of the crown and dust with a veil of cocoa powder. Transfer the St. Honoré to a large flat plate and serve at once. Use a very sharp knife to cut into slices at the table.

This impressive dessert represents the pinnacle of the patissier's craft.

makes 40 (to serve 8–10 as a lunch, 12–15 as a canapé)

1 quantity freshly made choux paste
(see pages 222–3), still warm
120g Emmenthal or Comté, grated
tiny pinch of cayenne pepper
pinch of freshly grated nutmeg
eggwash (1 egg yolk mixed with 1 tbsp milk)

mushroom duxelles
60g butter
500g button mushrooms, finely chopped
40g shallot, finely chopped
300ml double cream
2 tbsp snipped parsley
salt and freshly ground pepper

For the mushroom duxelles, melt the butter in a frying pan over a medium heat, add the mushrooms and cook, stirring occasionally, until their liquid has evaporated. Add the shallot and cook gently for another 2 minutes, then pour in the cream and cook for a further 5 minutes. Stir in the parsley and season to taste. Transfer the duxelles to a bowl, cover and stand in a bain-marie to keep warm.

Preheat the oven to 180°C/Gas 4. Line a baking sheet with greaseproof paper. For the gougère mixture, add three-quarters of the grated cheese, the cayenne and nutmeg to the warm choux paste and mix to combine, without overworking.

Place the gougère mixture in a piping bag fitted with a 1cm plain nozzle and pipe small mounds in staggered rows onto the prepared baking sheet. Brush with eggwash and lightly mark the tops with the back of a fork, then sprinkle over the rest of the cheese. Bake for 20 minutes until dry and crisp on the outside and base, but still soft inside.

Transfer to a wire rack. Using a knife tip, carefully cut a small hole in the base of each gougère. Put the warm mushroom duxelles into a piping bag fitted with a 1cm plain nozzle and pipe it into the gougères through the hole in the base. Serve immediately.

For a simple lunch, I serve these gougères with a lightly dressed salad of dandelion leaves and treviso. They are also perfect for canapés.

Original and light yet creamy, these delicious savoury éclairs are always popular. In the summer I often include them in an alfresco buffet.

makes 18 (to serve 9)

1 quantity freshly made choux paste
  (see pages 222–3), still warm
eggwash (1 egg yolk mixed with 1 tbsp milk)
4 oranges
bunch of watercress, trimmed and well washed
36 prawns, cooked and peeled, tails left on
salt and freshly ground pepper

orange mayonnaise
400g mayonnaise (see page 288)
juice of 2 oranges

For the mayonnaise, pour the orange juice into a small pan and bring to a simmer. Let bubble gently until reduced to 3 tbsp, then tip into a small bowl and leave to cool. Mix the cooled orange juice with the mayonnaise.

For the éclairs, preheat the oven to 180°C / Gas 4. Put the choux paste into a piping bag fitted with a plain 1.5 cm nozzle. Line a baking sheet with greaseproof paper. Pipe 18 choux bars, each 10 cm long, onto the baking sheet, spacing them 5 cm apart. Brush with eggwash. Cook the éclairs for 25 minutes until dry and crisp on the outside, but still soft inside. Place on a wire rack to cool.

Cut away the peel and pith from the oranges, holding them over a bowl to catch the juice. Cut out the segments between the membranes and add to the bowl with the juice. Set aside one-third of the smallest and most attractive watercress leaves for the garnish; snip the rest of the leaves.

To assemble the éclairs, slit them open along one side using a serrated knife, making sure you don't cut them completely in half. Mix half the orange mayonnaise with the snipped watercress and season with salt and pepper to taste. Spoon into the éclairs and spread evenly. Dunk the prawns in the remaining mayonnaise and arrange two in each éclair, leaving the tails protruding. Add a couple of orange segments and a few of the reserved watercress leaves to each éclair.

Serve the savoury éclairs on individual plates, allowing two per person.

There are good and bad pizzas, just as there are good and bad omelettes, but a really good pizza is a joy to eat. An excellent dough, made using the right flour (ideally French type 55) is important. Then once you've mastered the technique of making the dough and rolling it out, the rest is easy. A special thin wooden pizza slice is a useful tool for transferring the rolled-out dough to a baking sheet. Toppings can vary with the seasons and your own tastes. They may be completely or partially cooked on the base, or added after the pizza comes out of the oven. Good-quality olive oil and flavourful tomatoes are the two benchmark ingredients. I use fresh tomatoes when they are in high season, but at other times I prefer good quality tinned peeled Italian plum tomatoes (pomodori pelati). My favourite toppings are seafood and Provençal vegetables, but the most important element is the thin, perfectly cooked base.

pizza dough

pizza dough

makes about 1 kg

1st stage
450g type '55' flour or bread flour
330ml water
20g fresh yeast

2nd stage
20g fine salt
25g caster sugar
50ml extra virgin olive oil
120g type '55' flour or bread flour

The first stage Put the flour into a bowl and check the temperature. Now register the air temperature, and add the two figures. Together with the water, the sum should be about 64°C. So, for example, if the combined flour and air temperatures is 50°C, then the water needs to be at 14°C. If it's too cold, heat it; if too warm, add some ice cubes to chill to the correct temperature. Make a well in the flour and crumble in the yeast. Pour in a little water and mix with the yeast. Gradually add the rest of the water, mixing with the fingertips of one hand.

Continue to mix until you have a homogeneous, smooth dough. Cover with cling film and leave to rise in a warm place (20–24°C) for 8–12 hours.

The second stage On a lightly floured surface, punch the dough with one hand while folding it over itself with the other. Use one hand to add the salt, sugar and olive oil, a little at a time, and finally add the flour.

Mix well and knead until the dough becomes elastic, has some body and is slightly sticky to the touch. Cover with cling film and leave at room temperature for 1 hour. It will then be ready to use.

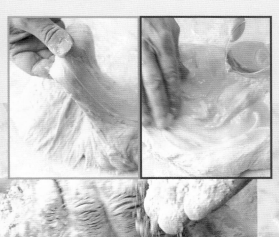

This dough makes a perfectly light base for any pizza. I have Fabio Ciervo, our Italian sous-chef at The Waterside Inn, to thank for revealing his secret recipe. He always cooks his pizzas in a non fan-assisted oven.

As you transfer the dough round, you may find that it shrinks a little, so dip your fingertips in flour and push the dough back to its original diameter.

On a lightly floured surface, roll out the dough thinly to a round (of the size suggested in the recipe). Lightly flour the dough, lift the pizza base disc over your rolling pin and carefully transfer it to a baking tray or pizza stone if you have one.

illustrated on previous page

220g pizza dough (see pages 242–3)
100g cherry tomatoes, whole or halved,
   depending on size
60ml extra virgin olive oil, plus extra to drizzle
salt and freshly ground pepper
200g good-quality tinned Italian plum tomatoes
   (pomodori pelati)
100g mozzarella (preferably buffalo), cut
   into 2cm cubes
24 small basil leaves

Put the cherry tomatoes in a bowl, pour on the olive oil, season lightly and leave to marinate for about 20 minutes. Pass the tinned tomatoes through a mouli into a bowl. Season the puréed tomatoes with salt and pepper and drizzle with a little olive oil.

On a lightly floured surface, roll out the pizza dough to a 28cm diameter disc. Lightly flour the dough, then roll it loosely over the rolling pin and unroll it onto a baking sheet or pizza stone. With floured fingertips, push the dough outwards to make a perfectly round, evenly thin base.

Preheat the oven (preferably non-fan) to 200°C/Gas 6. Use a spoon to spread the puréed tomatoes over the pizza base in an even layer, then arrange the marinated cherry tomatoes and cubes of mozzarella evenly on top. Bake for 18 minutes. Use a palette knife to slide the pizza onto a wire rack and scatter the basil leaves over the top.

Transfer to a wooden platter or board and serve immediately, grinding a little pepper over the pizza as you slice it.

This classic pizza never fails to please. When I'm in the south of France, I serve little portions with an aperitif of local rosé wine or pastis.

serves 8

420g pizza dough (see pages 242–3)
3 tbsp groundnut oil
80g butter
6 medium onions, about 750g, very thinly sliced
100ml double cream
about 9 thyme sprigs
salt and freshly ground pepper
3 unsmoked bacon rashers

Heat 2 tbsp oil with the butter in a shallow pan. Add the onions and cook over a medium heat for 10 minutes, stirring from time to time. Lower the heat and continue to cook very gently for about 20 minutes. Add the cream and the leaves from 3 thyme sprigs, and cook for another 10 minutes. Season to taste and set aside.

For the pizza bases, divide the dough into 6 equal parts and roll each into a ball. Roll the balls into 10 cm discs, about 5 mm thick, and place on a baking sheet; the dough may shrink as you do this, so dip your fingertips in flour and push it back to its original 10 cm diameter. Divide the onions between the pizza bases and spread to within 5 mm of the edge. Leave to stand for 10 minutes.

Preheat the oven (preferably non-fan) to 200°C/Gas 6. Bake the pizzas in the hot oven for 20 minutes. Just before they will be ready, fry the bacon rashers in a non-stick frying pan until crisp or soft, as you prefer. Drain on kitchen paper and cut each one in half.

As soon as the pizzas are cooked, transfer them to a wire rack. Top each one with a piece of bacon and the rest of the thyme sprigs, broken into short lengths.

Serve immediately, with a salad of frisée or other bitter leaves.

pissaladières

serves 4

200g pizza dough (see pages 242–3)
100ml light olive oil
800g onions, very thinly sliced
2 garlic cloves
1 bouquet garni (to include a few oregano
   sprigs and fennel stalks)
salt and freshly ground pepper
18 anchovy fillets, soaked in milk for an
   hour if salty
40 small black olives (preferably Niçoise)
1 tsp tiny thyme sprigs

Heat the olive oil in a heavy-based saucepan. Add the onions, garlic and bouquet garni, and season very lightly with salt. Cover and cook very gently over a very low heat for 2 hours, stirring with a wooden spoon every 20 minutes and making sure that the onions do not colour. When meltingly tender and lightly confit, tip them into a bowl, discarding the garlic and bouquet garni. Leave to cool at room temperature. Drain off any excess oil.

On a lightly floured surface, roll out half the pizza dough to a 28 x 12 cm oblong. Lightly flour the dough, then roll it loosely over the rolling pin and unroll it onto a baking sheet. Dip your fingertips in a little flour, then press the dough all over to make a very thin, even base. Repeat with the other piece of dough and rest in the fridge for 20 minutes.

Preheat the oven (preferably non-fan) to 200°C/Gas 6. Use a fork to spread the onions lightly and evenly over the pizza bases. Arrange the anchovies in a lattice over the onions, and put the olives in the middle of the lattices (leave Niçoise olives whole; cut larger olives into pieces). Bake for 10 minutes, then immediately scatter over the thyme sprigs. Use a palette knife to slide the pissaladières onto a wire rack.

If necessary, neaten the edges of the pissaladières with a knife, and cut each one into four. Serve piping hot, allowing two pieces per person.

Serve for lunch or as a snack, or cut into small fingers for canapés.

This pizza is a real feast – vary the fish according to what is available.

220g pizza dough (see pages 242–3)
8 fresh mussels, cleaned
8 fresh clams, cleaned
8 raw prawns
4 raw langoustines
60g fresh tuna fillet
60g fresh swordfish fillet
60g baby squid pouches, cleaned and
    cut into rings

100ml extra virgin olive oil, plus extra
    to drizzle
salt and freshly ground pepper
200g good-quality tinned Italian plum
    tomatoes (pomodori pelati)
80g mozzarella (preferably buffalo),
    cut into 1cm cubes
1 tbsp flat leaf parsley leaves

Steam the mussels and clams until opened, then shell, leaving 2 or 3 of each on their half-shell. Peel the prawns, leaving one in its shell. Shell the langoustines and halve the tails lengthways. Cut the tuna and swordfish into 2cm cubes and place in a bowl with the prawns, langoustines and squid. Pour on 80ml olive oil, season lightly and mix gently, then add the cooled shelled mussels and clams. Set aside to marinate for about 20 minutes.

Pass the tinned tomatoes through a mouli into a bowl. Season the puréed tomatoes with salt and pepper and drizzle with a little olive oil.

On a lightly floured surface, roll out the pizza dough to a 28cm diameter disc. Lightly flour the dough, then roll it loosely over the rolling pin and unroll it onto a baking sheet or pizza stone. Dip your fingertips in a little flour, then push the dough outwards to make a perfectly round, evenly thin base.

Preheat the oven (preferably non-fan) to 200°C/Gas 6. Using a spoon, spread the puréed tomatoes in an even layer over the pizza base. Arrange the marinated seafood, raw fish and mozzarella on top, and place the unshelled prawn in the centre.

Bake for 20 minutes, then arrange the mussels and clams in the half-shell on the pizza and return to the oven for 2–3 minutes. Scatter the parsley leaves over the top and slide the pizza onto a wire rack using a palette knife.

Serve at once, cut into slices. Hand round the pepper grinder, and extra virgin olive oil for drizzling. I also like to serve a salad of mesclun or other bitter leaves on the side.

provençal vegetable pizza

serves 8

200g pizza dough (see pages 242–3)
2 garlic cloves, thinly sliced
150ml extra virgin olive oil
4 baby aubergines
4 baby courgettes

16 cherry tomatoes
4 very tender baby artichokes, stems trimmed
salt and freshly ground pepper
180g mozzarella (preferably buffalo), diced
large handful of rocket leaves

Mix the garlic with the olive oil in a large bowl. Halve the aubergines, courgettes, tomatoes and artichokes, and add them to the bowl. Toss to coat in the oil and leave to marinate for 10 minutes.

Preheat the grill or barbecue. Using a slotted spoon, transfer the vegetables (but not the tomatoes) to the grill pan or barbecue and cook on all sides until charred and cooked, but still retaining some crunch. Season the vegetables and keep warm.

Roll out the pizza dough on a lightly floured surface to a 25 cm round, 1 cm thick. Transfer to a baking sheet or pizza stone; the dough may shrink as you do this, so dip your fingertips in flour and push it back to its original 25 cm diameter. Arrange the cherry tomatoes and mozzarella evenly on top and leave to stand for 20 minutes. Reserve the oil. Preheat the oven (preferably non-fan) to 200°C/Gas 6.

Cook the pizza in the oven for 20 minutes. Remove it and immediately arrange the grilled vegetables on top. Scatter over the rocket leaves and drizzle with some of the reserved olive oil. Serve at once.

With its colourful topping of baby vegetables, this pizza is delectable and, of course, you can adjust it to suit your taste.

These mini pizzas are perfect for drinks parties – the riot of colours and flavours is guaranteed to delight guests. Of course, you don't have to prepare all the toppings. You might prefer to choose three or four – increasing the quantities as necessary. All of the toppings and tomato coulis can be prepared a few hours in advance.

mosaic tapas pizzas

makes 42 (6 of each topping)

1.2kg pizza dough (see pages 242–3)
about 300ml olive oil, for the toppings

tomato coulis
50ml olive oil
150g onions, chopped
1kg tomatoes, peeled, deseeded and diced
40g garlic, chopped
1 thyme sprig
salt and freshly ground pepper

vegetable topping
6 miniature courgettes, blanched and sliced
6 miniature carrots, blanched
3 miniature fennel bulbs, halved and blanched
3 miniature aubergines, halved
3 tbsp tomato coulis (see above)
80g mozzarella (preferably buffalo), diced

prawn topping
6 prawns, preferably raw, peeled
3 tiny purple artichokes (the kind you can eat
    whole), stems trimmed and very finely sliced
18 broad beans, blanched and skinned
3 tbsp tomato coulis (see above)
80g pecorino cheese, grated

tuna topping
3 thumb-sized strips of fresh tuna
1 small onion, chopped
3 tbsp tomato coulis (see above)
1/2 medium onion, cut into rings
18 capers
6 small parsley sprigs, to finish

anchovy topping
6 raw anchovy fillets
fine salt and sugar, to marinate
3 tbsp tomato coulis (see left)
1 small red or yellow pepper, peeled, deseeded
    and diced
12 green olives, stoned and halved
1 tbsp pesto (see page 288, or use
    ready-made)
oregano sprigs, to finish

cherry tomato topping
12 small cherry tomatoes
80g mozzarella (preferably buffalo), diced
6 small basil sprigs, to finish

pata negra topping
6 small cherry tomatoes
80g mozzarella, diced
6 small thin slices of pata negra ham
12 rocket leaves
6 small Parmesan shavings

mushroom topping
40g pecorino cheese, grated
18 small girolles, grilled
3 small chipolatas, grilled and cut into thirds
6 tiny broccoli florets, blanched and grilled
rosemary sprigs, to finish

For the tomato coulis Heat the olive oil in a saucepan, add the onions and cook gently for 5 minutes. Add the tomatoes, garlic and thyme, and cook slowly for about an hour to make a thick coulis. Discard the thyme, whisk lightly and season to taste. Leave to cool. (The coulis can be kept in the fridge for several days, topped with a film of olive oil.)

illustrated on previous page

To prepare the toppings For the vegetable topping, brush the vegetables with olive oil and grill or griddle, turning, until tender; leave to cool. For the prawn topping, pan-fry the prawns (if using raw ones) in a little olive oil until just pink. Fry the sliced artichokes in a little oil and grill the broad beans until tender. For the tuna topping, sear the tuna strips in a very hot pan with a little olive oil until cooked 'rare', then remove and cut in half. Cook the chopped onion in a little olive oil for 3–4 minutes to soften, then add to the tomato coulis. Deep-fry the onion rings until crisp; keep hot. For the anchovy topping, marinate the anchovy fillets in a mixture of 90% fine salt and 10% sugar for 5 minutes.

To shape the pizzas Divide the dough in half to make it easier to roll out. Generously flour your work surface (ideally a cool one) and roll out the dough to a rectangle, 3 mm thick. Cut out 21 rounds with a 5 cm plain pastry cutter, or cut into 5 cm squares with a sharp knife. Put the rounds or squares on a baking sheet. Dip your fingertips in olive oil and lightly press the surface of each pizza to make them all even. Repeat with the rest of the dough. Preheat the oven (preferably non-fan) to 200°C/Gas 6.

To assemble the pizzas For the cherry tomato and pata negra pizzas, halve or quarter the tomatoes and arrange on the bases with the mozzarella. Spread a little tomato coulis on all the other pizza bases, except the mushroom ones. For the vegetable pizzas, top with the mozzarella and grilled or griddled vegetables. For the prawn pizzas, sprinkle with the pecorino and top with the artichoke slices and broad beans. For the tuna pizzas, arrange the capers on the coulis. For the anchovy pizzas, arrange the pepper on the coulis. For the mushroom pizzas, sprinkle the pecorino on the bases and top with the girolles, chipolatas and broccoli.

To bake the pizzas Place them on 1 or 2 large baking sheets and bake for about 10 minutes. As soon as you take them out of the oven, drizzle a few drops of olive oil on top of each one.

To finish For the pata negra topping, arrange the ham, rocket and Parmesan shavings on the bases. For the prawn pizzas, top with the prawns. For the tuna pizzas, top with the tuna and onion rings. For the anchovy pizzas, top with the anchovies, olives, a few drops of pesto and the oregano. Garnish the other pizzas with the herbs as suggested.

To serve Arrange the pizzas on a warm platter and serve hot or just warm.

serves 8

300g pizza dough (see pages 242–3)
80g provolone or pecorino cheese,
  cut into 1 cm cubes
60g small watercress or rocket leaves
2 tbsp extra virgin olive oil
salt and freshly ground pepper

polenta
70g quick-cook polenta
45g butter
1 tbsp light olive oil

For the polenta, generously grease a baking tray, using two-thirds of the butter. Heat 400 ml water in a saucepan with the olive oil, remaining butter and a good pinch of salt. As soon as it comes to the boil, add the polenta, stirring as you do so. Cook very gently for 10 minutes, stirring with a wooden spoon every 2 or 3 minutes. Pour the polenta onto the greased baking tray, leave to cool, then cover with cling film and refrigerate.

Preheat the oven (preferably non-fan) to 200°C / Gas 6. Divide the pizza dough into 6 equal pieces. On a lightly floured surface, roll one piece into a 3–4mm thick disc and place on a baking sheet. Repeat with the other 5 pieces. If necessary, dip your fingertips in a little flour and lightly press the discs to ensure that they keep their shape and thickness. Arrange the cubes of cheese on the pizza bases and bake for 10 minutes.

Meanwhile, cut the polenta into 1.5 cm cubes. Put 7 or 8 cubes on each pizza and return to the oven for 2 minutes. As soon the pizzas are ready, slide them on to a wire rack using a palette knife. Toss the watercress or rocket with the extra virgin olive oil, season lightly with salt and scatter on top of the pizzas. Grind over a little pepper and serve the pizzas straight away.

Polenta works really well on this pizza. You could use Cheddar instead of provolone or pecorino, though it won't give you quite the same result.

calzone

A folded pizza encloses a fragrant filling with lovely intense flavours.
Unlike most calzoni, the dough is fine and the filling is generous.

320g pizza dough (see pages 242–3)
200g cherry tomatoes, whole or halved,
    depending on size
200g sliced cooked ham, cut into 3cm squares
40 small basil leaves
60ml extra virgin olive oil
salt and freshly ground pepper
200g ricotta

For the filling, put the cherry tomatoes in a bowl with the ham and basil. Drizzle over the olive oil, season lightly and mix gently. Leave to marinate for about 20 minutes. Just before shaping the calzoni, crumble in the ricotta and toss gently.

Preheat the oven (preferably non-fan) to 200°C/Gas 6. On a lightly floured surface, roll out half the pizza dough to a 20cm diameter disc. Lightly flour the dough, then roll it loosely over the rolling pin and unroll it onto a baking sheet. Dip your fingertips in a little flour, then push the dough outwards to make a perfectly round, evenly thin base.

Spoon half the filling over one half of the base, leaving a 2cm margin. Brush the border with cold water and fold one half of the dough over the other, then press the edges together with your fingertips. Now, pushing the filling into the centre as you go, pinch the dough between your thumb and index finger, turning it 90° every centimetre to plait and seal the border.

Use the other portion of dough and remaining filling to make a second calzone. Bake for 20 minutes, then immediately slide onto a wire rack using a palette knife. Cut each calzoni in half and serve immediately.

There's a first time for everyone, even for me... Until recently, filo wasn't a pastry in my repertoire, so I decided it was time to master it. As you will see, the result was a great success and I now use it confidently to prepare amuse-bouches and canapés like parma ham mikados (page 271) and little crab triangles (page 272), as well as sweet dishes.

Paper-thin with a silky texture, filo is a wonderfully supple and malleable pastry, but it dries out and cracks if exposed to the air for more than a few minutes. The solution is to keep the sheets of filo you are using covered with a very lightly dampened tea towel, and to work quickly as you assemble the dish. You'll need to brush the sheets of filo with a light film of melted butter or olive oil depending on the recipe, and again just before cooking. Once baked, the pastry will be crisp and light. Of course, you can buy ready-made filo for convenience, but why not have a go at making your own?

filo pastry

filo pastry

makes about 780g (13 x 60g sheets)

As with all pastry, mastering filo is very satisfying, so I hope you will give it a try. The difficulty of rolling the dough to the required thinness of only 0.5mm is not insurmountable, but it's certainly a challenge.

Combine the flour, salt and water in the bowl of an electric mixer fitted with a dough hook and mix at low speed. As soon as the ingredients start to come together, pour in the oil in a thin stream.

400g plain flour
6g fine salt
330ml water, heated to 50°C
30ml olive oil
cornflour, to dust

Stop mixing as soon as the dough is amalgamated. Use a spatula to scrape down any dough sticking to the sides of the bowl and the dough hook. Switch the motor to medium speed and work the dough for 3–4 minutes. It will almost come away from the bowl when it is fairly soft and slightly sticky.

Put the dough on the work surface and shape it into a ball. Divide it into pieces about 60g each. Shape each piece into a ball and place on a baking sheet dusted with cornflour, spacing them several centimetres apart. Cover with cling film and leave to rest somewhere fairly cool (14 – 16°C if possible) for at least 2 hours before using the filo.

Lightly dust a 60 cm round wooden board with cornflour and place a ball of filo in the middle. Using a long, thin wooden pole (or piece of dowelling) as a rolling pin, roll it into a 14 – 16 cm disc. From this point on, press down with your hands on each end of the pole to stretch the pastry sideways. It is essential to keep dusting the top of the filo as you stretch it. As soon as the sheet of filo is the perfect thinness (0.5 mm), lay it on a baking sheet and immediately cover with a lightly dampened tea towel or cling film to prevent it from drying out.

Make another sheet of filo using another ball of dough. Dust the first sheet with cornflour, then place the second sheet on top and cover this sheet with the tea towel or cling film. Continue in this way until you've used all the pastry, covering the final sheet with the tea towel or cling film.

continued overleaf

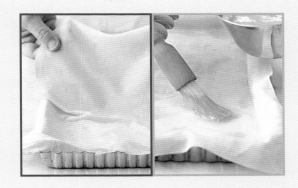

To use The pile of filo sheets can be refrigerated, well wrapped so that they don't dry out, if used within 24 hours. Brush off every trace of cornflour before using.

To freeze filo for later use Make sure that the filo sheets are tightly pressed together and wrap them very tightly in cling film, sealing it to make it completely airtight. Freeze for up to 2 weeks. Take it out of the freezer and refrigerate for 6–8 hours before using.

Ready-made filo This is usually sold in a roll consisting of a pile of 30 x 18 cm rectangular sheets. Of all pastries, filo is probably the most difficult to make, and while it's fun to have a go, you will probably find it much more convenient to use shop-bought filo. It keeps very well in the freezer or fridge. To familiarise yourself with the product, read the packet instructions. As with homemade filo, it is essential to keep the sheets covered with cling film or a tea towel to prevent them from drying out as you work.

Assembling filo Most recipes call for interleaving layers of filo. The sheets of filo will need to be brushed quite generously with melted butter or light olive oil as you pile them one on top of another, so have a bowl of melted butter or olive oil and a pastry brush to hand before you start to assemble the dish.

serves 8

6 sheets of filo pastry, 30 x 18 cm (see pages
   264 – 7, or use ready-made)
200 g spinach leaves
200 g sultanas
120 g butter, melted and cooled, or light olive oil
salt and freshly ground pepper
200 g fresh goat's cheese
2 red semi-confit peppers (see page 289)

Preheat the oven to 180°C / Gas 4. Blanch the spinach leaves in boiling water briefly until barely wilted, then refresh in cold water and drain well. Pat dry with kitchen paper. Blanch the sultanas in boiling water for 2 minutes, refresh in cold water, then drain well.

Brush a loose-bottomed 30 x 18 flan tin, 3 cm deep, with melted butter or olive oil. Very lightly brush a sheet of filo on both sides with butter or oil and place it carefully in the tin. Repeat with another 2 sheets of filo, laying them delicately on top of one other so that they are touching but not pressed together.

Season the spinach leaves with salt and arrange them on the filo base. Crumble over the goat's cheese, and scatter over the sultanas and strips of red pepper. Grind over a little pepper. Very lightly brush another sheet of filo with butter or oil and drape it over the filling. Repeat with the last 2 sheets of filo. Cut off the overhanging pastry with scissors, or fold it inwards over the filling.

Bake in the oven for 25 minutes until the filo is crisp and golden. Leave in the tin for 10 minutes, then push up the loose base to release the flan and transfer it to a wire rack. Serve on a platter and cut at the table with a sharp serrated knife. Because the pastry is so delicate, it will shed flakes as you cut it. Serve warm or cold, as a starter or light lunch.

Try varying the vegetables – asparagus, broccoli, mushrooms and tomatoes all work well. Pre-cook them before filling the flan.

makes 12

12 x 10 cm filo squares (see pages
   264 – 7, or use ready-made)
12 very small, thin slices of Parma ham,
   about 20g each
100g softened butter
30g strong Dijon mustard

Preheat the oven to 180°C / Gas 4. Cut each slice of Parma ham into fine julienne, keeping them separate. Mix the softened butter with the mustard and brush both sides of the filo squares very lightly with the mixture.

Lay a filo square on the work surface with one corner facing you and arrange one shredded Parma ham slice on top, crosswise to cover the filo. Lift up the corner nearest you and roll up the filo to enclose the ham, pressing to make a small roll the thickness of a pencil. Place on a lightly oiled baking sheet and repeat with the rest of the filo squares and ham.

Bake the mikados in the oven for 2 minutes. As soon as they are cooked, transfer them to a wire rack with a palette knife. Serve while still warm.

These little canapés are so delicious that they are likely to disappear quickly.
Serve three or more per person, with green and black olives.

filo crab triangles

makes 18

18 sheets of filo, 18 x 8 cm (see pages
   264–7, or use ready-made)
240g fresh white crab meat
finely grated zest of 4 limes
juice of 2 of the limes
4 red chillies, deseeded and very finely
   diced

40 coriander leaves, snipped, plus whole
   leaves to garnish
140g mayonnaise (see page 288)
salt
60g butter, melted and cooled
60 ml grapeseed oil (or groundnut oil)
sweet chilli sauce (ready-made), to serve

Combine the crabmeat, lime zest and juice, chillies, snipped coriander and mayonnaise in a bowl, and mix delicately with a spoon. Season with salt to taste.

Lay a filo rectangle on the work surface with a short side facing you. Brush a 1cm border all round the filo with melted butter. Put 1 tbsp (about 20g) of the crab mixture on the half of the rectangle furthest from you, placing it 4cm in from the top and side edges.

Fold the top left-hand corner over the crab, then fold the resulting filled triangle over, bringing the point to the bottom right-hand corner to make another triangle. Now fold the top right-hand point of this triangle down to the left-hand side of the filo, leaving an empty 1cm strip along the bottom. Fold this strip back over the base of the triangle and press to seal it well. Repeat with the other filo rectangles to make 18 triangles.

Heat half the grapeseed oil in a frying pan and fry 9 crab triangles over a medium heat for 1 minute on each side. Drain them on kitchen paper. Repeat to cook the other triangles.

Serve piping hot, garnished with a few coriander leaves and served with a separate bowl of sweet chilli sauce for dipping.

Bursting with fresh flavours and subtle spices, these crisp little filo parcels are the perfect appetiser. Allow three per person.

filo croustades with seared tuna

serves 4

20 x 10 cm squares of filo (see pages
  264–7, or use ready-made)
60g butter, melted and cooled, or light olive oil
1 tuna steak, about 160g
1 tbsp cracked white peppercorns
salt and freshly ground pepper
2 tbsp groundnut oil

30g butter
1 tbsp red wine vinegar
3 tbsp olive oil
80g rocket or mesclun leaves
8 cherry tomatoes, quartered
8 green olives, cut into thick matchsticks
2 hard-boiled eggs, each cut into 8 wedges

Preheat the oven to 170°C / Gas 3. Brush 4 filo squares on both sides with melted butter and use to line 4 individual quiche moulds, 10 cm in diameter and 3 cm deep. Now layer another 3 sheets of filo on top of the base layer, brushing the top of each one with butter and staggering them, so the points of each square are 2 cm from the one below.

Place an empty similar-sized quiche mould inside each filo-lined mould and press very lightly. Bake the croustades for 10 minutes. Remove the empty moulds as soon as they come out of the oven, then delicately lift the croustades out of their moulds and place them on a wire rack. (You can prepare these in advance, ready to assemble and serve.)

Sprinkle both sides of the tuna steak with the cracked white pepper and pat down with the flat of a chef's knife. Lightly salt the tuna. Heat the groundnut oil and 30g butter in a deep frying pan over a medium-high heat. Add the tuna and sear for 1 minute on each side if you like it rare, or 2 minutes each side for medium but still pink in the middle. Place the tuna on a small wire rack.

For the salad, whisk the wine vinegar, olive oil and some salt and ground pepper together to make a dressing. Use to dress the rocket or mesclun.

Place the croustades on individual plates. Divide the salad leaves, tomatoes, olives and hard-boiled eggs between them. Cut the tuna steak slightly on the bias into 4 slices and place a slice on top of each salad. Serve immediately.

serves 4

I love the contrast of the hot crispy quail legs and succulent cold breast meat in this refreshing dish. To serve it as a starter, halve the quantities.

8 sheets of filo, 16 x 8 cm (see pages
  264–7, or use ready-made)
2 oranges (preferably blood oranges)
2 tbsp groundnut oil
30g butter
4 oven-ready quails
2 tbsp clear honey

2 star anise
salt and freshly ground pepper
80g butter, melted and cooled
200g Greek yoghurt
4 small green spring onions, quartered
  lengthways
12 shredded mint leaves, plus sprigs to garnish

Peel the oranges, removing all white pith, then cut into segments between the membranes. Put the orange segments into a bowl and the membranes into another.

Heat the oil and 30g butter in a deep frying pan, add the quails and colour all over for 2–3 minutes. Pour off the fat. Coat the quails with the honey and add the orange membranes, star anise and 2 tbsp water to the pan. Season, then cover and cook gently for 12 minutes, basting the quails 2 or 3 times. Lift them out onto a plate and set aside to cool. Strain the cooking juices through a muslin-lined chinois into a bowl, pressing with the back of a spoon to extract all the flavours. You should end up with 3–4 tbsp full-bodied, syrupy jus.

When the quails are cold, cut off the legs and breasts with a knife. Remove the skin from the breasts and cut each one into 3 pieces. Place on a plate and cover with cling film. Using a knife tip, cut out the thigh bones from the legs.

Preheat the oven to 170°C/Gas 3. Brush one sheet of filo with melted butter on both sides, then cut lengthways into 4 bands, each 2 cm wide. Starting at the thigh end, roll the bands one at a time round one quail leg, to enclose it. Place on a baking sheet. Repeat with the rest.

Bake the filo-wrapped legs for 8 minutes just before serving. Meanwhile, gently warm the jus. Divide the yoghurt between individual serving bowls. Arrange the sliced quail breasts, orange segments, spring onions and a little shredded mint on top and drizzle the warmed jus over the quail breasts. Put the bowls on individual plates, place the filo-wrapped legs to one side, garnish with a mint sprig and serve immediately.

filo croustades with figs, almonds and fromage blanc

serves 4

Ripe white peach halves are an exquisite alternative to the figs in these elegant croustades.

**12 x 11 cm squares and 8 x 5 cm discs of filo
pastry (see pages 264–7, or use ready-made)**
80g caster sugar
**24 hazelnuts, lightly toasted, skinned and
roughly chopped**
80g butter, melted and cooled

1 egg, beaten with a pinch of salt
8 tbsp fromage blanc
4 perfectly ripe figs
**12 almonds (preferably fresh), skinned
and halved lengthways**

Put the sugar in a deep heavy-based frying pan and heat slowly until dissolved. As soon as it turns to a pale caramel, add the hazelnut pieces, roll them in the caramel, then tip the mixture onto a marble slab or lightly oiled baking tray. Use a knife tip to separate the hazelnuts, then set aside to cool.

To shape each croustade, very lightly brush 3 filo squares with butter on both sides, then cut each of the squares into 4 triangles. Brush a filo disc with melted butter on one side only and place it, buttered side-down, in an individual tart tin, 10 cm in diameter and 1.5 cm deep. Brush the top of the filo disc with beaten egg. Arrange the filo triangles evenly on the disc, each with a point facing upwards around the edge. Repeat with the other 11 triangles, bending them forwards slightly to resemble 12 'petals'. Finally, brush a filo disc with egg and place it, glazed side-down on the base of triangles. Brush the top with butter. Make another 3 croustades in the same way.

Preheat the oven to 160°C / Gas 2½. Bake the croustades for 5–7 minutes until they become dry and turn pale nut brown. Carefully unmould them onto a wire rack and leave to cool. (You can prepare these in advance, ready to assemble and serve.)

Place a croustade on each serving plate and divide the fromage blanc between them. Cut each fig vertically into 8 'petals', keeping them attached at the base, and open them out like a flower. Put one in each croustade and fill the centres with almonds. Scatter the chopped hazelnuts over the exposed fromage blanc and serve at once.

filo apple strudel

serves 6

illustrated on previous page

1 sheet of filo, 55 x 20 cm (see pages 264–7,
    or use ready-made)
100 g raisins
4 apples (preferably Braeburn or Cox's)
juice of 1 lemon
60 g caster sugar
1 tsp ground cinnamon
30 g icing sugar
whipped cream, to serve (optional)

For the filling, blanch the raisins in boiling water for 2 minutes, drain and refresh in cold water, then drain well. Peel, halve and core the apples, then cut each half into 2 mm thick slices. Place in a bowl with the lemon juice, caster sugar, cinnamon and blanched raisins. Mix gently, cover with cling film and leave to stand for 10 minutes.

Preheat the oven to 180°C/Gas 4. Lay the filo on a tea towel with one of the short edges facing you. Spread the filling evenly over the whole surface. Starting from the edge closest to you and using the tea towel to help, roll the filo into a sausage shape, enclosing the filling and applying light pressure as you go.

Carefully lift the rolled apple strudel onto the baking sheet and bake for 30 minutes until golden and crisp. Using a large palette knife, slide the warm strudel onto a wire rack.

Dust the strudel liberally with icing sugar and place on a serving platter. At the table, use a very sharp serrated knife to cut it slightly on the bias into 2.5 cm thick slices. Serve with whipped cream if you wish.

I used to make this with classic strudel pastry – stretching it carefully to avoid tearing until it was so thin you could read a newspaper through it.

16 sheets of filo, as large as your dish
  (see pages 264–7, or use ready-made)
400g pistachios, skinned
60g caster sugar
1 tsp ground cinnamon
140g butter, melted and cooled

syrup
250ml clear honey
80g caster sugar
pared zest of 1 lime
1 cinnamon stick
2 cloves

To make the syrup, put 160ml water in a heavy-based saucepan with the honey, sugar, lime zest and spices. Heat slowly to dissolve the sugar, then simmer for about 20 minutes until thick enough to lightly coat the back of a spoon. Strain through a chinois and keep hot.

To assemble, line a round or oval ovenproof dish, about 22cm in diameter, 5cm deep, with buttered non-stick baking parchment. Trim the filo sheets to the size of your dish. Blitz the nuts, sugar and cinnamon in a blender for 10 seconds until the nuts are coarsely chopped.

Preheat the oven to 170°C/Gas 3. Brush 6 sheets of filo on both sides with melted butter, and lay them one by top of another in the baking dish. Cover with half the coarsely chopped pistachio mixture. Brush another 4 sheets of filo with melted butter and lay them one by one over the pistachios. Cover with the rest of the pistachios. Brush the last 6 sheets of filo with melted butter and lay them one by one on the pistachio filling. Using a very sharp knife, cut the baklava into diamond shapes, cutting right through all the layers.

Bake the baklava for 15 minutes, then lower the oven setting to 150°C/Gas 2 and bake for a further 30 minutes. Let stand for 15 minutes, then ladle the hot syrup all over the surface of the baklava. Leave to stand for at least 12 hours (or up to 24 hours) before serving.

To unmould, slide a palette knife down the side of the dish and under the lining paper; it may help to run a cook's blowtorch under the base and round the outside of the dish. Lift the baklava out carefully onto a board and remove the paper. Using a very sharp knife, cut it into diamonds, following your original markings. Arrange on a platter or individual plates.

basics

béchamel sauce

serves 6

30g butter
30g plain flour
500 ml milk
salt and freshly ground pepper
pinch of freshly grated nutmeg (optional)

Melt the butter in a small heavy-based saucepan. Add the flour and cook gently for 2 minutes, stirring continuously with a balloon whisk to make a white roux.

Pour on the milk and mix with the whisk. Slowly bring the sauce to the boil over a low heat, whisking continuously. As soon as it comes to the boil, lower the heat. Let the sauce bubble very gently for about 5 minutes, stirring continuously and keeping the whisk in contact with the bottom of the pan.

Season the béchamel with salt and pepper to taste, adding a little nutmeg if you like, then pass it through a chinois. Serve immediately, or dot a few flakes of butter over the top of the sauce to prevent a skin forming, and keep it warm in a bain-marie.

hollandaise sauce

serves 6

1 tbsp white wine vinegar
3/4 tsp white peppercorns, crushed
4 egg yolks
250g butter, freshly clarified and cooled
   to tepid (see page 297)
salt
juice of 1/2 lemon

In a saucepan over a low heat, mix the wine vinegar, 4 tbsp cold water and the crushed pepper. Let bubble until reduced by one-third and leave to cool completely.

Add the egg yolks to the cold reduction and whisk to combine. Set the pan (on a heat diffuser if you have one) over a very low heat and continue whisking. Gradually increase the heat so that the sauce gradually emulsifies, becoming very smooth and creamy after 8–10 minutes. Don't let the temperature rise above 65°C.

Take the pan off the heat and, while still whisking, pour in the tepid clarified butter in a steady stream. Season with salt to taste. At the last moment, stir in the lemon juice and strain the sauce through a muslin-lined chinois to eliminate the grains of pepper (this is desirable but not essential). Serve immediately.

serves 6

2 tbsp white wine vinegar
30g shallot, finely chopped
3 tbsp snipped tarragon leaves
10 cracked white peppercorns
4 egg yolks
250g butter, freshly clarified and cooled
    to tepid (see page 297)
salt and freshly ground pepper
2 tbsp snipped chervil leaves

mousseline sauce

Prepare the hollandaise sauce (see left).
Just before serving, whip 75 ml whipping
cream to soft peaks and fold into the sauce
after the lemon juice. This is excellent
served with fish en croûte.

choron sauce

Prepare the Béarnaise sauce (see right) and
fold in 2 tbsp cooked tomato coulis. This is
another very good sauce to serve with fish
en croûte.

In a small heavy-based saucepan, combine
the wine vinegar, shallot, two-thirds of the
tarragon and the cracked pepper. Bring to
a simmer over a low heat and reduce the
liquor by half. Leave to cool completely.

Add the egg yolks and 3 tbsp cold water
to the cold reduction. Set the pan over a
very low heat (ideally use a heat diffuser)
and whisk continuously. The sauce should
emulsify and the temperature increase
gradually (never exceeding 65°C). Whisk
for 8–10 minutes until the mixture has
become rich and creamy.

Off the heat, whisk in the cooled clarified
butter, a little at a time. When it is all
incorporated, season the sauce with salt
and pepper, pass it through a chinois and
stir in the rest of the tarragon and the
chervil. Serve without delay. This is the
perfect accompaniment to beef en croûte.

mayonnaise

makes about 300 ml (serves 4)

2 egg yolks, at room temperature
1 tbsp strong Dijon mustard
salt and freshly ground pepper
250 ml groundnut oil, at room temperature
1 tbsp white wine vinegar or lemon juice

Put the egg yolks, mustard and a little salt and pepper into a bowl and stand on a tea towel on your work surface. Mix with a whisk to combine. Now slowly add the oil in a thin trickle to begin with, whisking continuously, then in a steady stream. When it is all incorporated, whisk more rapidly for 30 seconds, then add the wine vinegar or lemon juice and season with salt and pepper to taste.

Serve immediately, or cover with cling film, refrigerate and use within a few hours.

NOTE For a more pronounced flavour, replace some of the groundnut oil with a little olive oil.

For a richer, creamier mayonnaise, add 2 tbsp double cream after incorporating the vinegar or lemon juice.

pesto

makes about 300g

4 garlic cloves, green core removed
salt and freshly ground pepper
20 basil leaves
30g pine nuts, lightly toasted
100g Parmesan, freshly grated
150 ml olive oil

Pound the garlic with a pinch of salt to a purée, using a pestle and mortar. Still pounding, add the basil and toasted pine nuts and work until smooth. Add the Parmesan, then drizzle in the olive oil, using the pestle like a whisk. Season to taste.

Alternatively, you can make the pesto in a food processor. Put the garlic, salt, basil, nuts and Parmesan in the processor with half the oil. Blitz to a purée, then add the rest of the oil in a thin stream; the whole process will take 3 or 4 minutes. Season to taste.

Store the pesto in a screw-topped jar in the fridge with a thin layer of olive oil poured onto the surface to keep it fresh.

Use to fill my croissant baguette (see page 218), and with pasta, soups, vegetables, etc.

semi-confit tomatoes

makes about 700g

1 litre light olive oil
1 kg ripe cherry or medium tomatoes
2 thyme sprigs
1 bay leaf
2 garlic cloves (unpeeled), halved
15g white peppercorns, coarsely crushed

Heat the olive oil in a saucepan and add the whole, unpeeled tomatoes, thyme, bay leaf, garlic and crushed peppercorns. Cook gently at about 70°C for 5–10 minutes; the riper and smaller the tomatoes, the less time they will take to confit.

Leave them to cool in the pan, then transfer to a jar or bowl and pour over the oil. Cover with cling film and refrigerate until ready to use.

The semi-confit tomatoes will keep well in their oil for at least 2 weeks in an airtight container in the fridge. Just season them with salt and pepper before using.

NOTE These can be served as tapas, on toast, in pasta dishes and salads, or as a flan filling.

To serve them warm, pop them under a warm grill or heat for a few moments in a small saucepan with a little of their oil.

semi-confit peppers

makes about 400g

500g red, yellow or green peppers
  (or a mixture)
600 ml light olive oil
2 thyme sprigs
1 bay leaf
1 rosemary sprig
1 garlic clove (unpeeled)
1 tsp white peppercorns, coarsely crushed

Using your fingertips, lightly smear the peppers with a little olive oil. Grill them, preferably on a barbecue for the best flavour, until the skins burst and become blackened. Plunge into iced water to refresh, then remove and peel them.

Open up the peppers and remove the seeds and white membranes. Pat the peppers dry and leave whole or halve them. Heat the olive oil in a saucepan and add the peppers, thyme, bay leaf, rosemary, garlic and crushed peppercorns. Cook gently at about 70°C for about 30 minutes.

Leave to cool, then transfer the peppers in their oil to a jar or bowl. Cover with cling film and refrigerate until ready to use.

NOTE These taste even better if the peppers are grilled on a barbecue (I add vine shoots to the charcoal for extra flavour).

herb crêpes

makes 6 large crêpes

60g plain flour
150ml milk
2 eggs
salt and freshly ground pepper
15g chopped or snipped fresh herbs (flat
parsley, chervil, chives etc)
30g clarified butter (see page 297)

Put the flour into a bowl and make a well.
Add one-third of the milk, the eggs, a pinch
of salt and a grinding of pepper. Mix lightly
with a whisk to make a smooth batter,
then pour in the rest of the milk and mix
thoroughly. Pass the batter through a chinois.
Cover with cling film and leave to rest for
at least 30 minutes. Stir the herbs into the
batter just before cooking the crêpes.

Lightly grease a 26–30cm frying pan with
a touch of clarified butter. Give the batter
a stir, then ladle in just enough to cover
the base of the pan. Cook quickly for about
1 minute, then turn the crêpe over with a
palette knife and cook for barely a minute.
Repeat until you have used all the batter.

Stack the cooked crêpes on a plate, layering
a piece of greaseproof paper between each
one to prevent them sticking together.

I use these crêpes for my fillet of
beef in brioche crust and salmon
coulibiac; they form a protective
layer around the meat or fish,
keeping the pastry dry and crisp.
Of course, you can wrap them
around a savoury filling for an
easy supper.

sugar syrup

makes about 1 litre

750g caster sugar
90g liquid glucose

Put 650ml water in a saucepan, then add the sugar and glucose. Bring to the boil, stirring occasionally with a wooden spoon. Boil for 3 minutes, skimming the surface if necessary. Pass the syrup through a chinois and let it cool completely before using.

This sugar syrup (also known as stock syrup) can be kept in an airtight container in the fridge for up to 2 weeks.

candied citrus peel sticks

makes enough for 6–8 servings

2 grapefruit or large oranges
400g caster sugar
50g large-grain granulated sugar (optional)

Using a sharp, flexible knife, cut off a 5mm sliver from the base and top of the fruit. Starting from the top and following the contour of the fruit, cut off 5 bands of peel, 3cm wide and 6cm long, from each fruit (including the pith). Cut each band into 3 strips, each 1cm wide.

Put the strips in a saucepan, cover with cold water and bring to the boil. Refresh, drain and repeat the operation twice more.

Pour 300ml water into a saucepan, add the caster sugar and heat slowly to dissolve the sugar, then bring to the boil. As soon as the syrup boils, drop in the blanched citrus peel sticks and cook gently at 90°C for $1^{1}/_{2}$ hours.

Leave the citrus sticks in the syrup until barely warm, then lift out onto a wire rack and leave to drain until cold. If you wish, roll them in the granulated sugar. Store in an airtight container and use within 3 days.

crème anglaise

makes about 750 ml

500 ml milk
125g caster sugar
1 vanilla pod, split lengthways
6 egg yolks

Put the milk in a saucepan, add about two-thirds of the sugar and the vanilla pod and bring to the boil over a medium heat.

Meanwhile, whisk the egg yolks and the rest of the sugar together in a bowl to a light ribbon consistency. Pour the boiling milk onto the egg yolks, whisking continuously, then pour the mixture back into the pan.

Cook gently over a low heat, stirring constantly with a wooden spoon, until the custard thickens enough to lightly coat the back of the spoon (it should register 79.4°C on a sugar thermometer). Run your fingertip through the custard; it should leave a clear trace. Immediately take the pan off the heat.

Pour the custard into a bowl and leave to cool, stirring occasionally to prevent a skin forming. Pass through a chinois before serving. Once cold, the custard can be kept covered in the fridge for up to 3 days.

crème pâtissière

makes about 750g

6 egg yolks
125g caster sugar
40g plain flour
500 ml milk
1 vanilla pod, split lengthways
a little icing sugar or butter

Whisk the egg yolks and one-third of the sugar together in a bowl to a light ribbon consistency. Whisk in the flour thoroughly.

In a saucepan, heat the milk with the rest of the sugar and the vanilla pod. As soon as it comes to the boil, pour it onto the egg yolk mixture, stirring as you go. Mix well, then return the mixture to the pan. Bring to the boil over a medium heat, stirring continuously with the whisk. Let bubble for 2 minutes, then pour into a bowl.

Dust the crème pâtissière with a veil of icing sugar to prevent a skin forming as it cools, or dot small flakes of butter all over the surface. Once cold, it can be kept in the fridge for up to 3 days. Remove the vanilla pod before using.

chocolate crème pâtissière
Add 75g melted good-quality dark chocolate to the crème pâtissière before cooling.

serves 8

Adding double cream makes this vanilla ice cream extra rich and velvety, but it isn't essential. It's up to you to decide. For the best texture and flavour, serve soon after churning, or at least within a day or two.

1 vanilla crème anglaise (see left)
100 ml double cream (optional)

Pour the prepared crème anglaise into a stainless steel or glass bowl. Stand the base of the bowl in ice to accelerate the cooling, and stir with a wooden spoon or spatula from time to time to prevent a skin forming. When the custard is completely cold, remove the vanilla pod and add the double cream if you wish.

Pour the custard into an ice-cream maker and churn for about 20–25 minutes until the ice cream is firm but still creamy. Transfer it to a chilled freezerproof container, seal and keep in the freezer until ready to serve.

coffee ice cream
Dissolve 2 tbsp instant coffee in 2 tbsp hot water and leave to cool. Stir into the crème anglaise before churning.

italian meringue

makes about 600g

360g caster sugar
30g liquid glucose (optional)
6 egg whites

A sugar thermometer is essential when making this meringue. The liquid glucose prevents sugar crystals forming in the egg whites when you add the sugar syrup, which can otherwise make the meringue grainy.

Put 80 ml water into a heavy-based saucepan, then add the sugar, and glucose if using. Bring to the boil over a medium heat, stirring and skimming occasionally. Use a pastry brush moistened with water to brush down any crystals that form on the inside of the pan. Increase the heat and put a sugar thermometer into the boiling syrup. When it registers 110°C, lower the heat to minimum.

Keeping an eye on the syrup, beat the egg whites to stiff peaks, either by hand or in an electric mixer. The moment the syrup reaches 121°C, take the pan off the heat and let the bubbling subside for 30 seconds. Pour the syrup in a thin, steady stream onto the beaten egg whites, whisking at low speed.

When all of the syrup has been absorbed, continue to beat at low speed for about 15 minutes until the meringue is almost cold (30–35°C). It is now ready to use.

almond cream

makes about 1.1 kg

chantilly cream

makes about 600g

250g icing sugar
250g ground almonds
250g butter, at room temperature
50g plain flour, sifted
5 eggs
50ml rum (optional)

500ml whipping cream, well chilled
50g icing sugar or sugar syrup (see page 291)
pinch of powdered vanilla, or the seeds
   scraped from a vanilla pod

Sift the icing sugar and ground almonds together and set aside. In a large bowl, work the butter with a whisk until creamy. Still whisking, add the icing sugar and almond mixture, then the flour. When the mixture is evenly combined, incorporate the eggs one by one, whisking between each addition. You should now have a smooth, light cream. Stir in the rum if you wish.

This cream will keep in an airtight container or a bowl covered with cling film in the fridge for up to a week. Leave it at room temperature for 30 minutes before using.

Put the chilled cream, icing sugar or syrup and vanilla into the chilled bowl of an electric mixer and beat at medium speed for 1–2 minutes. Increase the speed and beat for another 3–4 minutes until the cream starts to thicken to a light ribbon consistency; don't overbeat it.

Chantilly cream is best used as soon as you have made it, but it will keep in a covered bowl in the fridge for up to 24 hours.

chocolate chantilly cream
Melt 150g good-quality dark chocolate in a bain-marie, taking care not to heat it above 45°C. Stir until smooth and allow to cool slightly, then fold into the chantilly cream.

coffee chantilly cream
Dissolve 2 tbsp instant coffee in 2 tbsp tepid sugar syrup (or use 1 tbsp liquid coffee extract) and add it to the cream before beating it.

NOTE For a smoother, looser cream, stir in 250–300g crème pâtissière (see page 292) at the last moment.

Bain-marie A water bath, used to control the cooking of custards etc., and to keep delicate sauces warm. A bowl over a pan of simmering or hot water functions as a bain-marie on the hob; for the oven a baking dish may be placed in a roasting pan containing hot water.

Bake blind To bake empty pastry cases, either partially or fully, before adding the filling. Line the pastry case with greaseproof paper and fill with ceramic baking beans or dried pulses before baking.

Blanch To plunge an ingredient (generally prepared vegetables) briefly into boiling water, usually for 30 – 60 seconds, then refresh in cold water to preserve their colour or parcook them.

Butter, clarified To prepare, melt butter very gently in a saucepan and then bring it to the boil. Ladle the clear butter through a muslin-lined sieve, leaving the milky deposit in the bottom of the pan.

Caramelise To heat sugar until it dissolves and forms a caramel. Also used to describe cooking foods until their natural sugars or a sugar topping has browned.

Chinois A conical strainer used to sieve a mixture to make it smooth.

Coulis A thin purée, usually of fruit mixed with a little sugar syrup, of a pouring consistency.

Crimp To pinch up the border of a tart with a pastry crimper or between your index finger and thumb.

Eggwash An egg yolk lightly beaten with 1 tbsp milk, used to lightly brush dough before baking.

Foncer To line a mould or tin with rolled-out pastry.

Glaze To brush or dust pastry or a tart filling with a mixture to give colour and shine. Eggwash is often used as a glaze. Icing sugar may be sprinkled over puff pastry, then caramelised in a hot oven to glaze.

Knock back To return risen dough to its original volume by lifting it with your lightly floured hand and quickly flipping it over 2 or 3 times.

Reduce To boil a liquor steadily to reduce and thicken it by evaporating some of the water.

Refresh To immerse food in cold water after blanching to stop the cooking process, preserving colour and texture.

Toasting nuts Place the nuts on a baking tray in the oven at 180°C/ Gas 4 for 10 minutes or until evenly coloured, shaking occasionally.

Zest To pare orange, lemon or lime zest with a zester very thinly, leaving behind all the bitter white pith.

Kitchen equipment
For perfect results, you need top-quality precision equipment. I use a Krups electric mixer; its built-in scales allow the ingredients to be weighed directly into the bowl, and the hook amalgamates the dough cleanly – essential for perfect pastry.

The frying pans, pastry moulds and loose-bottomed tart tins that I use have a non-stick Tefal coating, which I consider to be the best.

Global saucepans enable me to cook sauces, syrup, caramel and the like to perfection.

I buy my pastry rings and baking sheets from the professional cookware suppliers MORA in Paris; their equipment is durable and reliable: www.mora.fr

Special ingredients
Chocolate I always use Valrhona chocolate for my desserts, as it has a superb flavour. Chocolaterie Valrhona: www.valrhona.com

Fruit purées I use Boiron fruit purées, which are as intensely flavoured as any made using fresh fruits: www.boironfreres.com

Flours I use French type 45 and type 55 flours, obtainable from specialist suppliers, such as: www.shipton-mill.com

acknowledgements

It gives me pleasure to thank the
following people. Without their help
I could not have produced a book of
this quality:

Douglas Gregory, my head *tourier*
at The Waterside Inn, who helped
me to prepare the dishes for
photography with a rare enthusiasm
and expertise.

My special thanks to **Martin
Brigdale** who fulfils and even
surpasses my own aspirations.
His superb step-by-step photos
leave me lost in admiration.

Mary Evans who discreetly but
surely steers Martin and me
towards the perfect artistic results
she desires.

Kate Whiteman who translated
the French manuscript into English
with the same verve and accuracy
as in my previous books.

Janet Illsley who co-ordinated
the whole tight-knit team in this
marvellous undertaking to produce
a flawless book.

Claude Grant, my assistant, who
calmly and serenely typed and
edited the French manuscript along
with the other innumerable things
she has to do.

Robyn Roux, my wife, who patiently
checked all the English recipes,
even though I was sometimes
excessively demanding.